The crisis zone of Europe

The crisis zone of Europe

An interpretation of East-Central European history in the first half of the twentieth century

IVAN T. BEREND

Translated by ADRIENNE MAKKAY-CHAMBERS

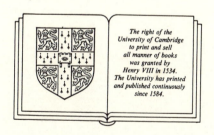

The right of the
University of Cambridge
to print and sell
all manner of books
was granted by
Henry VIII in 1534.
The University has printed
and published continuously
since 1584.

CAMBRIDGE UNIVERSITY PRESS

Cambridge
London   New York   New Rochelle
Melbourne   Sydney

Published by the Press Syndicate of the University of Cambridge
The Pitt Building, Trumpington Street, Cambridge CB2 1RP
32 East 57th Street, New York, NY 10022, USA
10 Stamford Road, Oakleigh, Melbourne 3166, Australia

First published 1986

Printed in Great Britain at the University Press, Cambridge

British Library cataloguing in publication data

Berend, Ivan T.
The crisis zone of Europe: an interpretation
of East-Central European history in the first
half of the twentieth century.
1. Central Europe – History
I. Title
943.08   D104

Library of Congress cataloguing in publication data

Berend, T. Iván (Tibor Iván), 1930–
The crisis zone of Europe.
Bibliography: p.
Includes index.
1. Europe, Eastern – History. 2. Central Europe –
History. I. Title.
DJK49.B46   1986   943   85–29994

ISBN 0 521 32089 5

WD

Contents

DJK
49
B46
1986

Preface

I am glad to be able to present this study to my English readers. I should begin by saying a few words about the origin of it. The initiative came from Cambridge University Press which, after my lecture series, generously invited me to publish the text of my Ellen McArthur lectures which I delivered at Cambridge University in the autumn of 1984.

The topic I decided to speak about after having received the invitation from Cambridge was the consequence of the semi-successful modernisation in nineteenth century East-Central Europe and the shock of both the successes and failures of it. This led to different types of revolts – Bolshevik revolution, national revolutions and right-wing radicalisms – in the first half of the twentieth century. As an economic historian I was, for a long time, challenged to analyse the consequences of economic–social processes on the general historical trends and to try to present, if at all possible, the complexity of history. I had begun work on this topic in the late 1970s: I published a book, *Decades of Crisis*, in Hungarian in 1982, and immediately continued the work having prepared a rewritten and further developed version with an English editor. I have been given the chance to work on the subject at

Preface

All Souls College, Oxford, and at the W. Wilson International Center for Scholars, Washington, which elected me to visiting fellow in 1980 and 1982–3, respectively.

It was a wonderful opportunity to be able to present my views on the interrelationship between economic, social, political, ideological and cultural history to an excellent Cambridge audience and, furthermore, to spend two very quiet weeks living in the Master's Lodge of St Catharine's College enjoying the unique intellectual atmosphere of Cambridge, which allowed me to think over some of the basic problems of my lecture series. After returning to Budapest, I used my notes to write this book, which was translated by Mrs Adrienne Makkay-Chambers.

I cannot mention here all my colleagues and friends who contributed to my work, but I should like to express my gratitude to Prof. Barry Supple, a very good friend of mine, who was my host in Cambridge and the initiator of my lecture series.

Budapest, September 5, 1985   IVAN T. BEREND

1 Failures of economic, social and national development

The peoples inhabiting the huge area of Central and Eastern Europe, which stretches from Germany to Russia and includes the regions of South-East Europe, have had a formative influence on world history. In this area started the two most devastating world wars so far in the history of mankind; here Nazism came into existence, grew stony, gained power and fell; here the communist revolution sprang up, became triumphant and created a new social order. With the break up of the huge multi-national empires, late national revolution led to the rebirth or creation of new, smaller states and to a considerable redrawing of the map of Europe. (After World War II a similar process took place in the 'third world', although geographically on a wider scale.)

People of the World War II generation, my generation, [John K. Galbraith wrote] will always think of their conflict as the great modern watershed of change . . . But we should know that, in social terms, a far more decisive change came with World War I. It was then that political and social systems, centuries in the building, came apart – sometimes in a matter of weeks. And others were permanently transformed. It was in World War I that age-old certainties were lost . . . The Age of Uncertainty began. World War II continued, enlarged and affirmed this change. In social terms

1

World War II was the last battle of World War I . . . The Eastern European scene is especially important for us. It was here, not in Western Europe, that the cracks in the old order first appeared. It was here that it dissolved, first in disorder, then in revolution.[1]

What was the reason for this powerful earthquake, this long-lasting crisis which brought the peoples of Central and Eastern Europe into such speedy and restless motion?

To find the answer I shall consider the joint processes of the economic, social, ideological, political and cultural history of Central and Eastern Europe, and analyse the subtle interactions which influence the processes of social change.

My starting point – as well as the subject of my first chapter – is the basic socio-economic element of these processes. Or, to put it another way, their antecedents, since in order to understand the first half of the twentieth century we have to go back to the events of the nineteenth century. (In this I am not trying to state that the movements under analysis started only in the nineteenth century, but the limits of these discussions do not make it possible to reach further back into history. I can mention very briefly only that the peoples of Central and Eastern Europe were 'latecomers' in European history; and that the River Elbe was in some mystical way already the border between Western and Eastern Europe in the last years of Charlemagne's Empire at the beginning of the ninth century, and again became the border in the peace arrangements after World War II. The Empire represented a Christian, feudal and agriculture-based Western world that was considered 'European'. As opposed to this, whatever lay east of the Elbe was barbaric and unsettled. Peoples appeared and disappeared in the last waves of the great migration. Central and Eastern Europe began to take firm shape in about the tenth century and to adopt Western institutions, concomitant with their conversion to Christianity. Between the tenth and fifteenth centuries the new countries started the hard and often hindered process of catching up with Western Europe: a process which they completed to different degrees and in various ways. At the turn of the fifteenth and sixteenth centuries, however, when the West began its spectacular and successful transformation into a modern world, the countries of Central and Eastern Europe fell behind disastrously. The rebirth of rigid feudal structures, or the introduction of them in places where they had not existed in their proper form before, refeudalised Central and Eastern Europe at a time when Western Europe had set out on the path of capitalist development. This happened in the Russian Empire, according to Soviet historians, and in the Rumanian principalities (where the serfdom-based feudal order was created only on the eve of the French Revolution). As opposed to the new economic tendencies of the West, production in this part of the world was still effected by masses of serfs working on the landlords' 'latifundia'. The system – often referred to as *Leibeigenschaft* in German historiographies – spread in the German, Czech, Hungarian and Russian territories, and turned the Central and Eastern European area into an agrarian periphery to a developing Western world.)

In addition to these medieval and early modern antecedents, new events occurred which did not favour the progress of these countries. At around the turn of the eighteenth and nineteenth centuries the industrial revolution in England and the social revolution in France (the two together were called the 'double revolution' by Eric Hobsbawn) brought about major changes: a fast industrialisation started, and a democratic social and political system was formed in Western Europe. Both these features were closely linked to a third: they strengthened the idea of nation states integrating various ethnic and linguistic groups which lived between the borders of a country into one state. Because of the differences in their internal development the countries of Central and Eastern Europe could not follow the path of the double revolution on their own in the first half or two-thirds of the nineteenth century, and so they fell even further behind the West. The widening of the gap is clearly illustrated by the following figures: according to Paul Bairoch, in 1800 the level of development on the basis of the gross national product *per capita* in the Western European countries was 7 per cent higher than the European average, whereas it was 5 per cent lower in the Habsburg Empire. In 1860, however, the Western European average was already one and a half times higher than the European average, whereas the level of the Habsburg Empire was 7 per cent lower. The growth of the difference is even more obvious when we compare the strictly defined Eastern European countries with Great Britain: in 1800 the countries of Eastern Europe stood 20 per cent below the European average and reached half the level of Great Britain. In 1860, however, they were 50 per cent below the European average, and had reached only one-third of the level of Great Britain.

Nicolai Bukharin rightly stated in his excellent but somewhat forgotten book *Imperialism and World Economy* that

the dichotomy between 'town and country', as well as the development of this dichotomy formerly confined to one country only, are now being reproduced on a tremendously enlarged basis . . . Entire countries appear today as 'towns', namely, the industrial countries, whereas entire agrarian territories appear to be 'country' . . . a few consolidated, organised economic bodies ('the great civilised powers') on the one hand, and a periphery of undeveloped countries with a semi-agrarian or agrarian system on the other.[2]

To use Arnold Toynbee's famous 'challenge and response' pattern we might say that the ever widening gap between East and West became a real challenge for those who remained behind. In a way, however, it was more than a challenge: it had great economic implications as well as the danger of dependency, and it also meant a social, political and even military threat to the peripheral countries. The economic changes that had taken place in the West increased the demand for food and raw materials, which caused world trade to increase nine-fold during an approximately fifty-year period in the middle of the nineteenth century. The sudden growth of world trade, however, did not affect commodities – according to the figures of Simon Kuznetz – or even the structure of foreign trade, or its geographical distribution. At the same time, the proportion of food and raw materials in world trade remained more or less unchanged at about two-thirds of the whole for almost half a century preceding World War I. On the other hand, Europe's share in world trade hardly decreased and was also steadily around two-thirds of the total amount. In other words, the peripheries of Europe which produced food and raw materials were furnished with great opportunities to transport these goods. They were able to multiply their exports in their traditional goods. The 'pull-effects' of the European market, therefore, offered enormous possibilities for the more backward countries. But the traditional patterns of production did not ensure the appropriate conditions for making the most of these possibilities.

The extension of the economic relationship, moreover, was also a threat: it meant an increasing subordination to the more developed and industrialised West.

The dangers were, nevertheless, even more threatening in the political and social field. Within the old-fashioned almost medieval political systems of Central and Eastern Europe, there was great attraction to the ideas of English liberalism and French rationalism and to the structures themselves built upon these theories in the West. The effect of these ideas and their practice was obviously enormous, and it not only fascinated the small intellectual circles of these backward countries, but also presented an example for the ruling conservative elite to follow in order to secure their power.

This became particularly important for them because of the military threat arising from the widening gap in development. The industrialised West grew far stronger economically, politically and militarily than the Central and Eastern European countries, even though there were huge empires among them, which thus made them more vulnerable. The balance of forces was overturned. Some countries could rightly feel that their independence was in danger. Others, such as the multi-national empires, saw their dominant political position at risk. The threat was recognised not only by historians of succeeding generations, but also clearly enough by contemporaries. Halil Pasha, commander of the army of the Turkish Empire (and, by chance, also the son-in-law of the Sultan) expressed his perception very clearly in his memorandum in 1830: 'If we do not follow Western Europe, we shall have no alternative but to go back to Asia.' This complex challenge required profound and comprehensive changes in response, which were promptly initiated. What took place in the area from Prussia to Russia within these decades can be regarded as an effort to respond to the Western challenge. The reforms were carried out step by step, and often took decades. They were directed from above, which was characteristic of Central and Eastern Europe. The pattern was set by Prussia, which started to introduce reforms in order to modernise the country almost immediately after the defeat they had suffered from Napoleon. The new measures were connected with the names of two men, Stein and Hardenberg, who brought about thorough changes, from the abolition of serfdom to the creation of several other requirements of the modern bourgeois state. The challenge of the Napoleonic wars for Prussia was most palpable and the response, therefore, was rapid. Militarised Prussia experienced the trauma of the defeat especially deeply. (Prussia was often ridiculed, not without reason, as an army with a state, instead of a state with an army.) The Czarist Russian Empire, which to its misfortune emerged triumphantly from the Napoleonic wars, did not even recognise the necessity of reform. A lost war necessarily preceded such a recognition. The defeat they suffered in the Crimean war had a stimulating effect from this point of view too, and called forth the reform of serfdom in 1861 relatively quickly as well as a series of other reforms which transformed administration of state and army in the 1860s and 70s. The Turkish Empire started to reform itself after the military defeat they had suffered in Greece. From the 1830s onwards the 'Tanzimat' reforms were introduced which, however, were not sufficiently radical.

The Prussian, Russian and Turkish examples were not unique. Similar reforms were introduced in almost all countries of the (Central and Eastern Europe) area, mostly in the 1860s. In some cases, for example in the Rumanian principalities, rulings laid down in the peace arrangements of the great powers contributed to the reform processes, whereas in other cases, for example in Hungary or in Congress Poland, suppressed fights for freedom were followed by (political) compromises and reforms.

Besides the response Central and Eastern Europe gave to the Western challenge in the form of internal reforms carried out from above, the rapidly developing system and institutions of international economic relations greatly assisted transformation to modernity of this backward area in the nineteenth century. One of the factors of these international relations was the export of capital, which grew to a greater and greater extent in the second half of the century, especially from the 1870s onwards. Part of the capital surplus pro-

8

duced in the more developed countries was directed to these backward countries with a low level of growth. The significance of this is shown by the fact that 40 per cent of the capital invested in Hungary between 1867 and 1913 was from Austrian, German and other external sources. More than half of the capital invested in Russian industry and, almost uniquely, 90 per cent of the investments in Rumanian industry came from abroad at around the turn of the century.

The imported capital contributed to the transformation of agriculture, to opening mines and establishing industrial plants. It had a particularly important role in the development of modern transportation networks. Approximately half of the capital brought into these countries from external sources was invested in building railways, so that even in this backward area there was an up-to-date railway network which was more highly developed than the general level of any individual country of the area. The length of railway lines relative to population and geographical area was not far from the Western European norm: since relatively cheap mass transportation was available, the backward areas were linked to the markets of the developed industrialised countries.

In the second half of the last quarter of the nineteenth century these countries become more and more involved in division of labour on an international scale by new institutions such as trade or low protective tariffs, the introduction of the gold standard, a standardised system of measures and other things which improved international economic relations.

As a result of this, the major difficulties were overcome so that these backward countries could use their opportunities for export. The traditional sectors, especially agriculture, started to develop relatively quickly. The agricultural production of the Central and Eastern European countries was eventually increased two- or three-fold during the fifty-year period before World War I because of the elimination of serfdom, the sufficient supply of capital and the adoption of up-to-date methods: the introduction of modern crop-rotation, improvements in crops, large-scale water regulation works, the mechanisation of agriculture and soil-improvement. As a result of this, at the beginning of the twentieth century Russia herself provided one-quarter to one-third of the world's wheat export trade; Rumania supplied 8 per cent of pork exports from Serbia; and cattle and corn exports from Hungary increased dramatically.

Where internal economic, social and cultural conditions were suitable, their interaction had an important role in altering the sectors of the economy. In Hungary, for example, the large-scale production and export of corn initiated the industrialisation of the 1860s, since it led to the development of an internationally significant food industry (particularly milling). While Italy and Rumania exported their corn almost exclusively in an unprocessed form, Hungary transported two-thirds of its processed corn in the form of flour. In the second half of the century Budapest became the second biggest centre in the world for the milling industry. Preconditions for Budapest's gaining such significance were not only sufficient capital, a spirit of enterprise and a class of entrepreneurs, but also an industrial background such as could supply the growing milling industry with machinery and which could undertake the improvement of milling technology. One of the most important engineering works in Hungary, the Ganz Works, which had been founded by a Swiss immigrant, played a major role in the technical advancement of the industry. Its Bavarian-born engineer and managing director, András Mechwart, invented a special cart rolling mill, and his patent enabled him to manufacture the most up-to-date milling equipment of the time for Hungarian mills. This guaranteed the Hungarian milling industry a competitive advantage in world markets in respect of both prime cost and quality. Thus, it is evident that, although the export of corn in itself did not ensure the beginning of industrialisation, through such suitable enterprises and their technical contribution it nevertheless became feasible. (The role of technical innovation in this case is very similar to that of the invention of the milk separator in Danish industry, which opened the way to development.)

In Hungary railway building also had far reaching effects. The first period was characterised by the import of rails, rolling-stock and engines. Initially import was the only means of satisfying the needs of the home market, but the products of the growing internal metal and machine industry gradually superseded imported goods, and by the end of the nineteenth century they created self-sufficiency in railway building and maintenance in Hungary.

In some more successful cases, then, the beginning of industrialisation emerged from an export trade based on traditional products and caused the economy to change to a modern structure. The degree to which changes in the structure of industry in the latecomer

Central and Eastern European countries took place, and the extent to which these changes led to the formation of modern economic structures, differed significantly from one country or region to another in Central and Eastern Europe.

Instead of analysing the processes in detail, I should like to describe the three major types of response made to the Western challenge in the field of industry and the structural changes in the economy.

The Western region of the area, above all Germany and also the Western part of the Austro–Hungarian monarchy beyond the Lajta, caught up with Western Europe successfully despite having started off late. During the last few decades of the nineteenth century Germany not only caught up with its Western European competitors, but, through particularly rapid industrialisation, overtook them; the Austrian and Czech areas also were approaching the industrial standards of the Western half of the Continent. As opposed to these successful cases, several countries of the area did not get to the point of industrial breakthrough, but remained in the backward agricultural, rural state.

Within the validity of this general statement, two types of 'failure-cases' can be distinguished: the semi-successful (or we could say semi-failure) cases, which include Hungary, the Polish areas and Russia; and the complete failure cases, which include mainly the Balkan countries (Greece, Rumania, Serbia and Bulgaria). In the former group, semi-success or semi-failure meant that the interference of effects resulted in some structural changes in industry, but that these changes did not yet lead to modern industrial structures. In the complete failure cases there was no interference of effects or developing structural change. The traditional sectors extended and exports increased in these countries, too, but the traditional structural pattern remained unaltered. Although the production of the most important export goods increased significantly in certain cases, it either required almost no modern industrial processing, or it hardly even made such activity possible. One of the most characteristic examples of this was the Greek export trade, 56 per cent of which consisted for a long time of a single item: raisins. The situation was similar for Serbian livestock or prunes, Bulgarian tobacco, or Rumanian corn. Naturally, the lack of a modern structure restricted economic development, and, in the countries unable to progress, even the receipt of foreign loans on a large scale (which was charcteristic of the backward areas) could not promote production in order to repay the loan or to achieve a sufficient surplus for export. Greece, Bulgaria and Serbia (the failure cases) lost their creditability, and at around the turn of the century went bankrupt one after the other.

Thus, Central and Eastern Europe produced three kinds of response to the Western challenge which were economically and also in other respects radically different from each other. Germany and the Austrian–Czech areas, Serbia and Bulgaria represented extremely diverse types of response. But most of them can be regarded as failure or semi-failure cases.

The Central and Eastern European response to the Western challenge, however, cannot be identified only with economic achievement. Structural changes in the economic field demanded radical changes in the social structure as well. The Central and Eastern European

13

countries could not, however, follow the Western social transformation as well as they could the economic and the structure of society remained more rigid and more backward than that of the economy. Social organisation and the pattern of attitudes and values remained far more traditional than the economic structure itself. Even if the gross national product per head increased considerably, the heads which owned it did not change to any great degree.

The countries of the area represent two in many ways similar but also significantly divergent types of social structure. The Balkan societies are rightly called 'incomplete societies'; that is to say in these countries the long (sometimes five-century) Turkish rule created societies which lacked a ruling elite or a modern middle class. Until the Turks were driven out of the Balkan countries, an almost entirely peasant population stood in opposition to a ruling Turkish elite. Following the late formation of the independent nation-states, middle classes and a new, independent ruling elite started to come into existence. The minor bourgeois elements naturally played some role in this, but basically the military/political elite which had taken part in the fight for independence, and the elite involved in the developing new state administration, became the determining factors of the process. Thus, power – as well as wealth – was, on the whole, concentrated in the hands of the bureaucratic/military ruling class, whilst the majority of the population, the peasantry, had got rid of their Turkish landlords and were part of the remaining village land communities; they did not generally lose their lands, but, since they owned tiny plots, continued to live in great poverty.

They did not reach the marked-oriented stage of farming, but 'vegetated' on the extremely poor, traditional, self-supporting dwarf holding. Rising from a peasant status was a rare exception. The middle class of the entrepreneurs was very weak. The means of climbing the social ladder or making one's fortune was not that of enterprise, but, traditionally (following the Turkish pattern), taking advantage of one's position in state administration in order to gain wealth rapidly; open corruption and speculation, a modern variant of the hated Turkish spahi-system. (The spahis, dependent on the Sultan, had their commission for an indeterminate period, so they tried to exact as much as they could from the villages and other areas under their control, since they were not sure how long they would keep their office. The new bureaucratic/military elite also aimed at making an immediate fortune, due to the uncertainty of the period of time they would be in power.)

The characteristic feature of the other types – the Prussian, Czech, Hungarian, Polish and Russian societies – was the continuing existence of an aristocracy in the period of modern capitalistic development. In the first place, we should remember that in these cases the nobility was a much larger social class than in Western Europe. While in pre-revolutionary France the nobility constituted only 1 per cent of society, in Hungary the figure was 5 per cent, and in Poland 10 per cent. In spite of the fact that the 1848 revolutions or the reforms carried out from above had abolished noble privileges and had laid the foundations of the modern bourgeois state, the old structures and social traditions persisted. Within the

15

framework of these traditions, the significance of birth remained crucial, and social status was determined by one's family. The Prussian junker, the Hungarian aristocrat or the Polish *szlachta* belonged to the upper class society and the ruling elite, even if he had lost his estates and had been reduced to poverty long before. His birth ensured him an upper class position in society, which was mainly accompanied by office in the state machinery, in the army, in the government, or in ministerial or county departments, even if in some cases in positions of low rank. Business, trade, industry, or any sort of enterprise, was considered a despised 'Jewish' activity by this social class. The entrepreneur's role was not attractive for them, and they looked down on the puritan ethics of developing capitalism. Their retrograde anticapitalism, their prodigal and parasitical way of life and their system of values influenced not only the attitude of the members of these classes but became an attractive ideal in general, and became a rigid but nevertheless much-imitated pattern for the rising elements of society whose customs, way of life and thinking were strongly affected.

The aristocracies, however, were characterised not only by a ruling elite and a special middle class gentry but by a peasantry whose social status was determined by the two classes above them. In other words, in these societies the peasants were not part of the aristocratic system; as in the classic feudal state, they were excluded from society. In spite of modern capitalist development, this exclusion persisted stubbornly. Rising financially and becoming rich were not sufficient to allow the peasant to advance from his inferior social status. The peasant masses who represented the great majority of society were excluded from most spheres of society, from politics to education, and rising from their low status was exceptional.

Hence, the rigidity of the noble societies was hindered from both above and below from forming the modern middle classes, the entrepreneur class and the modern bourgeois state in general. Thus, a peculiar vacuum was created in the central spheres of society. In many cases, this vacuum was filled only by people who were outside society. It was due to this that in most countries of Central and Eastern Europe, alien elements took up trade, banking, industry and enterprise. In some cases and in some countries it was Greeks or Germans, but for the most part Jews dominated these professions. In Rumania, Poland and Hungary one-third to one-half of those involved in trade, industry and banking were Jewish, and the proportion was even greater among people running large enterprises. The modern world of business and capitalism was built into these societies as an alien element.

In spite of the fact that the 'incomplete societies' of the Balkan and the Central and Eastern European noble societies greatly differed from one another in several respects, they showed basic similarities as well; above all in the fact that instead of the modern middle classes and the ruling elite, there was a special bureaucratic military–junker elite. Political power was unquestionably in the hands of this group, who used it also for developing a considerable influence on economic life.

The responses these countries gave to the Western

17

challenge may have been very different in the economic field (contrast the German success and the spectacular failure of the Balkan countries), but from the social point of view the changes that had taken place in these countries showed fewer divergencies. Germany, the most successful economically, which had caught up with and surpassed England and France in industrial-isation, nevertheless shared many features in the social field with the more backward countries of the area. Economic development was too rapid to upset the less flexible social structure at once. The existence and extraordinary influence of this bureaucratic (a peculiar substitute class or *Erzatzklasse* as the Germans called it) junker–military elite continued to characterise German society.

Although the Central and Eastern European features of social development were apparently mostly in the Eastern German areas, in Mecklenburg and Prussia, German unification, the realisation of the so-called 'small-German principle' and the undisputed Prussian hegemony in a sense made Prussian features characteristic of the whole German state. As one of the most significant German political thinkers of the age, Heinrich von Treitschke, put it:

The whole Empire is based historically and politically on the fact that it is (as Kaiser Wilhelm once said to Bismacrk) 'an extended Prussia', that Prussia is the dominant factor, both in fact and in formula. What is our German Imperial Army? Unquestionably it is the Prussian Army . . . extending over the whole Empire . . . The conditions are such that the will of the Empire can in the last instance be nothing else than the will of the Prussian State.[3]

Thus, even if it seemed that the German or Czech

areas had successfully caught up with Western Europe in the economic field, they had certainly not done so socially. And it was the same with the third decisive factor of modern bourgeois transformation, with national development. In spite of the fact that Bohemia and Moravia were the most industrialised and richest parts of the Austro–Hungarian Empire (after the break up of the Empire, they inherited three-quarters of the industrial capacity of the areas beyond the river Lajta), they did become an independent nation-state. Germany, as Bismarck put it, fought with fire and iron (or as J. M. Keynes, added: rather with coal and iron) in order to create a modern unified German Empire, although it is significant that it only became possible extremely late – in the 1870s. The fact that the development of the unified nation-state had been hindered for such a long time and that the Empire came into existence so late had several consequences. As has been described above, this fact influenced social development and had an effect on mass psychology. It also had a practical consequence, namely that national unity came into being too late for Germany to take part effectively in the 'empire-building' competition of the wealthy industrialised powers. Economic success was, for this reason, almost counter-productive. While Germany became the strongest industrialised power of the continent, it was not admitted into the club of the colonial powers. The feeling of humiliation, hurt and exclusion was particularly deep, precisely because of this contradiction. Hence, in German political think-ing it became predominant and decisive, i.e. taken for granted, that the future of the German people depended on the creation of an empire. Heinrich von

Treitschke formulated the idea in a most concise way in 1887 when he said that the future of a nation relied on its creating an empire, and if it could not achieve this, its future was hopeless.

It is hardly disputable that this peculiar lateness and distortion of Central and Eastern European development or, more precisely, its social and political features and consequences, played a crucial role in Germany's attempt to change its status and make its success complete in catching up with its envied Western rivals through war. However, the hopes engendered by war had been finally and completely shattered by the autumn of 1918. Instead of the victory that the whole nation longed for and considered to be certain, the country suffered a serious defeat. It lost Alsace-Lorraine, which it had acquired relatively recently; it was humiliated by being obliged to pay enormous reparations (as so many Central and Eastern European countries had done before, it ran into debts instead of becoming the proud creditor), and it had to bear the French occupation of the Rhine area. All this not only symbolised the loss of hopes about the war, but reinforced fears about being rebuffed and forced to retire to the periphery.

As a result of all this, in the countries of Central and Eastern Europe – even in case of the most recent successful economic response to the Western challenge – there grew up a powerful feeling of failure, bitterness, discontent, inferiority and being forced to the periphery. Failure in catching up with the fortunate and successful Western European countries and mass disappointment became the seed-bed of revolt. Whereas earlier they wanted to copy Western notions and institutions, now they started to regard them as more and more hateful and so increasingly stood out against them. From the turn of the century they wanted to follow and copy the West less and less; rather they denied its notions, destroyed its institutions, set up new ideals and rules, and sought new ways all the more. It was a revolt which manifested itself through ideology and fine arts first.

2 Ideological–cultural revolution

The Central and Eastern European countries' feeling of being pushed to the periphery prepared the ground for the revolt against liberalism, the free-market economy, parliamentary democracy and the rationalism of the Western world. It should not be forgotten that the rationality of the existing world-system was working against them, because it represented the ruling position of others; therefore, this world-system was no longer rational for them, and they turned against rationalism. Since they could not imitate the overall transformation of the West successfully, they started to deny the new values of this transformation. The revolt started to emerge at about the turn of the century, and gradually became more and more powerful and obvious during the thirty years from the 1880s to World War I.

Naturally, the roots of the whole movement reached deep down below the surface, just as they would in the case of any social or political process. In fact, the ideological revolt started very early; it was almost simultaneous with the triumph of the English industrial revolution. The first comprehensive criticism of English liberalism and free trade, the denial of Adam Smith's notions and their replacement with another concept, appeared in Johann-Gottlieb Fichte's book *Der Geschlossene Handelsstaat* (*Closed Commercial State*), only a quarter of a century after *The Wealth of the Nations*, i.e. in 1800.

This work is the conscious antithesis of Smith's concept. Whereas Smith expected economic and social harmony and national increase of wealth through individual freedom, Fichte sharply opposed such liberal ideas considering them unsuitable for solving the problems of backward countries. Smith postulated the existence of certain mechanisms which created balance by the help of an 'invisible hand' in the free-market activity. David Ricardo, in his later theory of comparative advantage, saw this harmony ensured for everybody through foreign trade between rich and poor, industrial and agrarian countries. At the turn of the eighteenth century in Germany, Fichte no longer believed in harmony and development created by an 'invisible hand'. For this, according to his theory, the backward countries needed a much too visible hand: the intervention of the state, and, what is more, the omnipotence of the state. In his *Der Geschlossene Handelsstaat* the key words most often appearing are *Gesetz und Zwang* (law and compulsion). Not the free movement of the individual, but the comprehensive and conscious activity of the state is necessary:

it is the State alone that unites an indeterminate multitude of human beings into an enclosed whole, into a totality ... The deeper-lying duty of the state ... is to install each (citizen) in the position suitable to him. It is only possible to achieve this last, however, if commercial anarchy is removed, if the state encloses itself as a commercial state in the same way as it has been enclosed with regard to its legislative and judiciary functions.[4]

23

Fichte's idea was the creation of a heavily central-ised, planned autarkical economy. In this respect, all spheres and activities of production and trade would be under the strict control and direction of the state.

All direct traffic by the citizen with any foreigner should be absolutely done away with . . . and moreover must be made impossible . . . All world-currency (such as gold and silver), which is in hands of citizens, should be taken out of circu-lation and exchanged against a new land-currency, i.e. one which would only be valid inside the country . . . The amount of foreign trade will be fixed (and) with every year imports must lessen. From year to year the public will need less of those (foreign) goods which can be produced in the country.[5]

Roland Butler, in his book entitled *Roots of National Socialism*, which appeared in 1941, describes Fichte's theories by saying: 'This embryonic German socialism is national-socialism.'

Such a categorical statement cannot be accepted. In my view, the Fichtean system has several aspects. It is not by chance that German social democracy also recognised its ancestor in it after World War I. When *Der Geschlossene Handelsstaat* was published again in Jena in 1920, Professor Waentig clearly made this point – in a similarly categorical manner – by saying that Fichte was the first social democrat. This view is not entirely groundless if we take into consideration the theoretical and practical tendencies of the German social democratic movement which developed in the spirit of the so-called 'organised capitalism' theory after the war.

Fichte's work, however, is characterised by a diver-sity of subsequent interpretations, since, for example, any Eastern European reader of *Der Geschlossene Handelsstaat* would consider it to be the spiritual antecedent of the Stalinist economic concepts of the 1950s.

Even if Fichte's ideas had a surprisingly colourful and diverse after-life, one thing can be firmly stated; that is that his notions were adopted as the political philosophy of the revolt which took place in the more backward countries against English liberalism and its universality. Due to the character of this political philosophy it could be attached to several kinds of revolt, and could become the spiritual forerunner of extremely diverse notions of revolution. In trying to find some further roots, however, we should consider not only Fichte's ideas. Just as the system of liberal concepts developed further during the nineteenth century, the Fichtean notions found followers as well. On the liberal side, David Ricardo and J. S. Mill extended Adam Smith's system by adding newer and newer stages of concept to it until about the middle of the century. The Fichtean notions formed a basis for ideological trends which rejected liberalism, justified state intervention and aimed at replacing international free trade with protectionism. One of the works representing these trends very clearly was Friedrich List's *Das Nationale System der Politischen Öconomie*, which appeared in 1841. The German author criticised Smith's 'cosmopolitanism', his ground-level 'materialism', extreme 'individualism' and 'particularism'. In List's system, the most important role is taken up by the national state which is between the individual and the world economy. The driving force of economy has to support national purposes. This economic nationalism was, as List consciously put it, the weapon of those countries which remained in a state of relative backwardness. Moreover, as a result of the special lateness of German development, even the rationale for founding an empire appeared in his work, together with an emphasis on the necessity of supplementary (*Ergänzungsgebiete*) territories.

With this I am not suggesting that there was an unbroken connection between the antirational and antiliberal trends from the beginning of the nineteenth century to the first half of the twentieth century. I would be particularly cautious in regarding the revolt against the English and French notions – in philosophic or economic theories – as a consistent development of some pre-fascist system. In reality, these spiritual trends had several implications simplified in the interpretation of the previously mentioned works by Butler and George Lukács, respectively.

To analyse the roots in detail would, however, require going further back into the past, which would break the strict chronological order of the process. So let me refer to the most characteristic elements of this ideological revolt at the turn of the century instead; first *inter alia* to Enrico Corradini's 'national socialism'. (With him, though, I step out of the strictly Central and Eastern European area, including a new, South-East European feature in the analysis. This 'frontier outrage' can, however, hardly be condemned theoretically since the Italian processes, and the historical development of the Mediterranean in general, show a basic similarity to the Central and Eastern European one. In this case, too, the failures or semi-failures, the dissatisfaction and the feeling of being on the periphery dominated. Here, too, we are faced with the breakdown of a backward country's attempts to catch up with the West, and with the reaction to a semi-successful modernisation.)

In E. Corradini's works the national ideology of rebellion appears to be a national ideology as in List's or Fichte's systems. Corradini was, however, the child of a modern era, and when building his ideological system he turned to Marx for material, which he used arbitrarily. The Marxists and socialists, he reasoned, saw the solution guaranteed in class struggle. In reality, however, class struggle does not take place within one nation, but between several nations. There are, he says, bourgeois nations and proletarian nations. These latter can rise from low status only through war against the rich, 'bourgeois' nations. But for this, unity must be created within the nation, the class opposition of nations must be brought to an end, and, as Corradini put it, syndicalism and nationalism must prevail. The first almost complete draft of this theory, and the use of the 'national socialism' action in Corradini's works, can be seen already in 1910. As students of the field rightly point out, Mussolini, who had started off from the socialist movement, had no need to do more than take and use this theory which had been born at the beginning of this century. It is not very difficult to realise the connection between Corradini's theory and the practice of the Italian fascist state, which attempted to link syndicalism and nationalism within the so-called corporative system. The chief purpose of the corporate state was, said the declaration of the manufacturers' fascist federation,

that of correcting and neutralizing a condition brought about by the industrial revolution of the nineteenth century

27

which dissociated capital and labour in industry, giving rise on the one hand to a capitalist class of employers of labour and on the other to a great propertyless class, the industrial proletariat. The juxtaposition of these classes inevitably led to the clash of their opposing interests.[6]

Although Corradini's ideas show a direct connection with the practice of Italian fascism, it is necessary to point out the ambiguity which springs from the source of revolt even in his system. It becomes particularly obvious if we consider the appearance of Corradini's notions in Turkey. There, the idea of rising through the fight between poor and rich countries lacks the pre-fascist view, and is exemplified in the deeply democratic Turkish revolution of Kemal Atatürk. During the period between the two world wars ideologists in the immediate circle of Kemal and later the next president, Inönü, reinterpreted Corradini's views, and by doing so they also altered them to a certain degree. They did not set out to correct Marx, but rather to complement his system. They accepted the Marxist class-struggle theory, but they regarded it as applicable only to rich, developed countries. At the same time, they emphasised that much as class struggle is the spring of historical development and the only means to further progress for the rich, industrialised countries, it is not, however, suitable for ensuring the rise of backward countries. Such a rise first demands struggle against the exploiting bourgeois nations by the poor proletarian nations. Hence, the class struggles within and among nations complement one another. It is worth noticing that in the circles of Kemal Atatürk, the ideology of the third world – to use a recent term – appears in a conscious, explicit way.

At about the turn of the century, however, other ideologies of rebellion came into view. Among these, particularly with regard to their popular power and influence, the *Völkisch*, *narodnyk* and *népies* movements occupied an important place. These three (German, Russian and Hungarian, respectively) terms mean the same and can be translated into English with one word only, i.e. 'populist'. In spite of this, these populist movements show basic differences. It is true, though, that each of them was fundamentally characterised by turning against capitalism. But while the Russian *narodnyks* discussed the possibility of avoiding the full development of capitalism and aimed at forming the future Russian socialism from the traditional persisting and flourishing *obshtshina*/village (land) communities, the German *Völkisch* movement rejected not only capitalism but socialism as well, and claimed a third, mystical and extremely nationalistic way, combined with the myth of race and blood. The later-emerging Hungarian *népies* movement, typically enough, soon broke up into two wings: a revolutionary-democratic, socialist-oriented one and another one which sank into anti-Semitism and sympathised with Nazism.

The general feature of the populist movement was, however, ethnic 'purity', the rejection of 'alien' elements, which was basically the source as well as the process of anti-Semitism. Such notions as the *Völkisch* movement led easily to the creation of the *Volksfremde* (national-alien) category concerning the non-German, chiefly Jewish population of Germany. Parallel to this, the famous formula of the leading ideologist of the early Nazi movement, Gottfried Feder, which distinguished between the Aryan producing industrial capital (*schaffendes Kapital*) and the Jew exporting financial capital (*raffendes Kapital*), was introduced just as easily. Here, the revolt against capitalism turned clearly against the Jews, and capital is seen as good or bad according to the person it belongs to.

Thus the *Völkisch* notions led almost directly to Nazi theory. Pan-Germanism, which was closely linked with the *Völkisch* movement, had a similarly direct connection with Nazi expansionism.

The populist rebellion prepared the ground for the different nazi movements, and brought into existence those pre-fascist ideological systems whose realisation these movements fought for. One of the most typical manifestations of the populist–fascist rebellion could be seen in Rumania. The charismatic leader of the 'Iron Guard', Corneliu Zelea Codreanu, was one of the most characteristic representatives of this ideology and movement; let me quote some representative pronouncements which were born in the spirit of the rebellion against Western values, and which could be found in some form or another in almost all the countries of the area.

Democracy breaks the unity of the Romanian people, dividing it into parties, stirring it up, and so, disunited, exposing it to face the united block of the Judaic power . . . Democracy transforms the millions of Jews into Romanian citizens, by making them the equal of Romanians . . . Democracy is incapable of continuity of effort . . . One party nullifies the plans and the efforts of another . . . Democracy is incapable of authority. It lacks the power of sanction . . . Democracy is in the service of great finance.[7]

'Human rights' are not limited only by the rights of other

humans but also by other rights. There are three distinct entities: 1. The individual. 2. The present national collectivity, that is the totality of all the individuals of the same nation, living in a state at a given moment. 3. The nation, that historical entity whose life extends over centuries, its roots embedded deep in the mists of time, and with an infinite future. A new great error of democracy based on 'human rights' is that of recognizing and showing an interest in only one of these three entities, the individual; it neglects the second or ridicules it, and denies the third . . . 'Human rights' are no longer unlimited, but limited by the rights of national collectivity, these in turn being limited by those of the nation.[8]

Zeev Sternhall was right when he stated in his *Fascist Ideology*: 'for the author of *Mein Kampf* had nothing to say which had not already been said'.[9] The pre-fascist and Nazi theories had emerged from the differently motivated right-wing radical movements and trends, but, from the turn of the century onwards, became politically practical, and then, between the two world wars, bloodstained reality.

There was, however, another major type of revolt, which not only denied liberalism and the parliamentary system, but also rejected capitalism itself. At around the turn of the century the link between Marxism and the problems of backwardness became manifest.

Karl Marx and Friedrich Engels, having analysed the contemporary development of capitalism and drawn their conclusions, predicted that since the progress of historical development was unstoppable the proletarian revolution would be triumphant; socialism would expropriate private property and create economic and social justice. This they expected to

31

happen as a consequence of the development of capitalism to its highest form, and particularly of the common revolutionary transformation of the most developed countries. From the last few decades of the nineteenth century and the turn of the century the classical Marxist concept of the proletarian revolution and socialism found itself at variance with not only the new processes of capitalist development, but also the unfolding revolt, the increasing revolutionisation of the more backward areas, especially of the Central and Eastern European countries. In this latter area the rebellion against the prevailing conditions, the rejection of Western values, the programme of a future promising harmony and improvement instead of failure or semi-failure, became associated with the Marxist critique of capitalism and with the notion of socialism as a matter of course. For this, however, Marxism had to be altered and refined so that, taking the conditions of backward countries into consideration, the Marxist system could be applied to a programme which would lead out of backwardness. This process started in the ideological transformation which could be described shortly as the birth of Marxism–Leninism. The start of the process was associated, ironically enough, with Karl Kautsky, who was later denounced as a renegade by Lenin. Kautsky was a typically Central European figure of the second generation in the Marxist movement and ideology: he was born in Prague; his father was Czech, his mother German. He was educated in Vienna and later became the leading theoretician of the German workers' movement. He became aware of the conflict between Marxist ideology and the problem of backwardness through the struggle of the German social democratic movement. The basic conflict was caused by the agrarian and peasant problem. For Marx, this question did not exist, since he was thinking in terms of a highly developed capitalist society; and, taking his examples from English experience, he regarded the agrarian and peasant problem as out-of-date from the point of view of the proletarian revolution and socialism. In the contemporary peasantry he already saw the future industrial proletariat, and anticipated that only a diminished and concentrated agrarian sector would persist. By Kautsky's day, however, it was impossible to neglect the problem raised by the presence of the significant masses of peasants even in German society, and the workers' movement realised the necessity of taking up a position on the agrarian and peasant problem. Thus, Kautsky, dealing with the agrarian issue, took the first steps in forming the attitude, the strategy and the tactics of the Marxist workers' movement over the burning questions of the backward countries. Kautsky's activity was, at one point, of pioneering significance in interrelating the problems of backwardness. This point was related to the new processes of capitalist development, i.e. to the phenomenon of imperialism, which he was one of the first to analyse. In his writings he discussed the new features of capitalist development at the turn of the century and (while doing so) he pointed out 'natural' attempts of developed capitalist countries to annexe agrarian territories.

It was this point which led much later to connecting the problems of backwardness to Marxist theory in the works of Rosa Luxemburg. She emerged from the

33

Polish socialist movement, but wrote her fundamental work about the accumulation of capital when already a teacher in the school of the German social democratic party. Her explanation, which was initially orthodox Marxism, substantially modified the Marxist view of primitive accumulation, which had been described in the famous twenty-fourth chapter of the first volume of the *Das Kapital*. Whereas primitive accumulation with Marx is the first and single act of capitalist development, in Luxemburg's view a capitalist economy constantly demands the expropriation of non-capitalistic sectors as a result of its fundamental character. Small-scale producers in developed countries and the whole non-industrialised, backward 'third' world are the suffering subject of this constantly recurring process of accumulation and expropriation. In this interpretation, there is a constant need for a 'third person' (to use Luxemburg's terminology) to advance capitalistic development and this so-called enlarged reproduction. Consequently, the inevitable conclusion drawn from this theory was that the agrarian peripheries under discussion, which were the victims of imperialistic expansion and were permanently exploited, inevitably became revolutionised, and their revolt linked up with the struggle of the proletariat against capitalism in the developed industrialised countries.

The most important thinker to adapt Marxism so that it should match the requirements of the backward countries was V. I. Lenin. In his book *The Development of Capitalism in Russia*, which he wrote in exile in Siberia at the end of the nineteenth century, he argued the *narodnyk* point of view. Then his major thesis was still that the backward, agrarian Russia could not avoid the path of capitalist development and, consequently, could not evolve into some kind of peasant socialism; this was especially true because the Russian economy, and even the Russian village, had already become fundamentally capitalist, and as a result of this the situation was ripe for a proletarian revolution even in backward, rural agrarian Russia. In a whole series of his later works, e.g. in the one about the two tactics of social democracy, or *What is to be done?*, or the ones written about imperialism, he created a framework for the theoretical and party-organisational-tactical requirements of the proletarian revolution in backward countries with systematic logic and close reasoning. In connection with this he argued the traditional social democratic view which suggested that the backward countries should go through a modern capitalist transformation first, i.e. they should go through all the processes of Western industrialisation involving economic, social and political changes to arrive at the proletarian revolution and later at the possibility of socialism. According to Lenin, these backward countries need not follow this route because they could achieve socialist transformation by a revolution which created a 'revolutionary democratic dictatorship' led by a small proletariat and could continue towards socialism through a permanent revolution. In other words, the twentieth century does not require a strict chronological order: the bourgeois, democratic revolution does not necessarily have to come first and be followed by the proletarian, socialist revolution. A combination of the two can lead the backward countries to socialism, instead of their following the West.

Lenin – contrary to and, moreover, at issue with Luxemburg – drew the consequences of this for the organisation of the workers' movement and the structure and functioning of the Marxist party. While Luxemburg had already connected Marxism with the problems of the backward world and the agrarian peripheries as regards the functioning and organisation of the social democratic party, she was still relying on democratic mass movement traditions. Lenin realised the contradiction of this notional system; namely, since the proletarian revolution and the possibility of change to a special socialism became realisable in the revolutionised backward world (to use Lenin's terminology, the 'weak links of imperialism'), the social democratic movement had to adapt its organisation and functioning to these circumstances. The democratic mass movement in these countries was impossible particularly because of their backwardness. The despotic systems were in fundamental opposition to a democratic movement. (In Germany, Bismark's special laws against social democracy were only temporary, but the Russian Empire outlawed democratic mass movements permanently and with strict consistency.) Particularly because of this, an entirely new type of party had to be set up, which was organised on an almost military basis; it was consistently centralised and had iron discipline; it was to prepare for the revolution (if necessary, by conspiracy), and was to mobilise and revolutionise the masses even in semi- or fully illegal circumstances.

That is why Lenin regarded the breach with the traditional social democratic movement and its international organisation, the Second International,
unavoidable, and it is why he found necessary the
establishment of an independent Bolshevik type party,
which took the Marxist–Leninist point of view. This
process was first realised in the Russian workers'
movement. The 1903, then the 1905, London, and
eventually the 1912 Prague congresses of Russian
social democracy developed and made the breach complete, and also created a Communist (Bolshevik) party
in the spirit of the aims and organisational theory of
Lenin.

Thus the ideology of the great rebellion which completely rejected capitalism, and the movement based
on it, was already born in the spirit of Marxism–
Leninism before World War I. It was able to turn its
notions into reality during the war and particularly
from the end of the war, and called forth the rapid
development of similar parties and movements after
1917.

The spirit of revolution, however, did not conquer
only the fields of ideology and practical politics.
Rebellion sprang up with great force in a special sphere
of social activity, which was, nevertheless, of particular importance in the Central and Eastern European
countries: in fine arts. It should not be forgotten that in
these socially and politically backward (consequently
autocratic–despotic) regimes, social activity was often
possible only in a transmitted form, and the criticism
of conditions and the attempt to transform them could
not prevail in conflicts between parties, could not
assert itself in parliamentary debates, and as a result it

37

often found an easier opportunity for self-realisation in the more abstract form of art. Thus, the artistic rebellion is not simply a 'reflection' of some growing dissatisfaction or mass mood: it is in itself social criticism.

If I wish to give a comprehensive picture of this artistic rebellion which swept through the countries of Central and Eastern Europe with elemental force, then I have to make a few introductory remarks in order to avoid the danger of being partial. First of all, the artistic revolution developing at about the turn of the century was not in the least an exclusively Central and Eastern European phenomenon. The great transformation of arts is far too universal and inseparable from revolutionary changes in the scientific concept of the world. These were the decades when the principles of Newtonian physics – due to the new discoveries – were no longer adequate for the full explanation of the physical phenomena of the world. While the laws of the macro-world were interpretable through them, the micro-world, particularly the phenomena of light-waves, seemed to follow some other rules, seemed to be comprehensible only with the help of some other principles. The concept of space and time changed, and several decades had to pass before quantum mechanics was able to offer a homogeneous explanation.

Discoveries in physics made the general concept of the world uncertain and contradictory, only to offer certainty on a higher level of perception. Thus, the discovery of X-rays made the human body transparent as did Sigmund Freud's great discovery about the subconscious, and Weismann's revolutionary discovery in genetics shok previous firm beliefs and gave new interpretations of mankind. The staggering processes of uncertainty and new discoveries necessarily brought a crisis and revival of the arts with it.

Emphasising the universality of artistic development, one should also mention the long processes and different periods of change. The transformation of the 'old' into the 'new' took place by almost infinite stages. The roots of the twentieth century artistic rebellion reached back into the nineteenth century. In the 1840s, i.e. sixty–seventy years before the first non-figurative abstract paintings or the futurist rebellion, William Turner, the painter of romantic sea storms, painted his *Sunset over the Lake*, an abstraction of light effects in which an orange–red dash of colour dissolves on a white surface; or *Rain, Steam and Speed* in which a rushing train emerges from the misty whiteness of the picture.

Naturally, other fields of art show similarly endless and gradual changes. The heights of romantic music opened the door to the disintegration of traditional musical structures, to the destruction of traditional harmony and ideals. Examples of this gradual process can be found in Richard Wagner's robust music, which, according to Mark Twain's witty remark, is 'not as bad as it sounds'; in the late works of Franz Liszt; in Debussy's new, dreamy, alienating voice; and even in Puccini's life-work, which follows and later surpasses the nineteenth century genre of opera.

The transformation of the arts was so universal and so gradual that it is obviously impossible to confine the analysis to the Central and Eastern European area. Far be it from me therefore to make parochial statements. The cultural history of the early twentieth century, however, clearly suggests that the Central and Eastern European rebels played a particularly important role in the great changes of art at that time. They were impetuous, they denied the micro-world that surrounded them, and consciously or instinctively they created their new art, the art of rebellion against traditional values. (As I have already mentioned, the Mediterranean countries were, in many respects, in a situation similar to that of Central and Eastern Europe. Thus, it can hardly be regarded as accidental that – especially in Spain and Italy – both political thinkers and artists had a significant role in the ideological and artistic rebellion, respectively.)

It often happens that an idea or feeling manifests itself in an artistic form before it appears in political or philosophical thinking. This manifestation is, in most cases, instinctive and lacks conscious intention. (Although sometimes the opposite is true: a conscious philosophy, or artistic programme, guides the pen or the paintbrush.) As the Russian Larionov put it in 1913: 'We are in opposition to the West, because it oppresses the East, because all values have lost their meaning there.' Thus, the destruction of the traditional ideals of harmony and beauty in Western art was often the conscious aim and philosophy of artists in the backward countries. The Italian futurists for instance (to cite a Mediterranean example again) expressed their aims very explicitly when they said that they wanted to pull down the museums and set the libraries on fire, and when, from their stagnant backward world, they praised speed, new technology, aggression and war.

This ideology was, understandably, close to that of

the Russian futurists, who, even though they were contemporary with their Italian associates, did not know of their existence. From an artistic point of view, they wanted to redraw the slogan and ideology of Russian revolutionary anarchism, i.e. 'Destruction is also creation'. In 1912 Mayakovsky, Kruchonikh and Hlebnikov expressed their opinion in their manifests in the following way: 'Only we are the face of our times ... the part is restricted. The Academy and Pushkin are incomprehensible. Pushkin, Dostoyevsky and Tolstoy should be thrown out of the steamboat of the present.'

Based on conscious philosophy or on artistic instinct, an overwhelming attack was made against traditional art in Central and Eastern Europe at the beginning of the century. Not only did new literary tendencies gain ground to break up traditional literature in these countries, but writers in Vienna and Prague gave voice to something that had never been mentioned before. The Viennese Musil, drawing on his own experiences at the military academy, wrote about the sufferings of Zögler Törless with cold-blooded passion. With this, in 1906, he forecast a microcosm, the world of torture and mutilation, of human defencelessness and humiliation, which was due to come very shortly. A similar defencelessness appeared in Kafka's works. Kafka came from Prague, the city of subtle contradictions, which inspired him to picture the irrationality of this world. Prague was the centre of politically oppressed Bohemia, which was, however, economically the most developed area of the multinational Austro–Hungarian monarchy. At the time it had a mixed population of mainly Czechs and Germans, but Kafka belonged to a Jewish minority whose feelings of exclusion and inferiority he showed. In his books power appeared to be faceless and impersonal. The individual, staggering hopelessly along to his destiny, found himself threatened, lost and defenceless in this huge irrational system.

In fact, neither Musil nor Kafka rebelled against the system; they only showed the irrationality of the world with endless bitterness. And soon came those years which proved that the absurdity of *The Palace* and *The Trial* was deep reality.

The literature of the Central and Eastern European countries was, perhaps, the first to produce this antiliterature of the absurd which only became really fashionable and set a worldwide trend after decades. Between 1908 and 1912 the Rumanian Demetrescu-Buzan (publishing under the pseudonym Urmuz) created half-human, half-marionette characters, and used such linguistic automatism as a vehicle for parody of literary cliches and conventions. In 1914–15 Tristan Tzara, I. Vinea and A. Manik were shocking their readers with non- or antiliterature. This was already a break with traditional literature, and in it half-finished sentences and meaningless texts dominate the writing.

These experiments, aiming only at shocking people, did not produce great literature. It is true, though, that not even the artists themselves were attempting to do so. They protested against the hated traditions and hated rationality. Goethe made a well-known remark about Byron that he was great only when he wrote poetry, but that when he responded to something he remained a child. In a sense the reverse of this is true for these writers: even if their art often remained childish, their reaction, their rebellion was significant.

Rebellion was more powerful and more noisy in music. The twentieth century revolution in music unquestionably started off from Central and Eastern Europe. The giant trio, the Viennese Schöenberg (the son of a Saint Petersburg opera singer), Ivor Stravinsky and the Hungarian Béla Bartók – each working independently of the others – launched a triumphant assault on the old harmony, old ideals and the old concept of beauty. How paradoxical it is that the rebellion started in Vienna, the very centre of traditional music, the capital of waltz, the world of Johann Strauss, Lehár and the Austro–Hungarian operetta breathing the false harmony of the 'golden, olden days'. It was in this Vienna, in 1907–8, that Arnold Schoenberg composed his first new pieces which suddenly broke the harmony of the flowing melodies which had been in fashion at the beginning of the century. In 1908 the Viennese audience received Schoenberg's String-quartet no. 2 with shock, laughter and mockery. From this time on his music became harsher and harsher, discords were left unresolved, tunes broken, and his music became a cry, a scream. As the contemporary Ernst Křenek justly stated later: 'The catastrophe, which was on the doorstep, was clearly predicted in this music.' However, Schoenberg should, perhaps, in the first place be appreciated as a philosopher and innovator–theoretician. In 1910–11 in his writings on harmony he expounded the theoretical foundations of his musical experiments and his radical breach with the traditional view of harmony. Schoenberg broke with the diatonic scale which characterised baroque and romantic music so much, and perhaps his greatest artistic achievement was the negation of all previous

43

music and the creation of a new language and structure. In his works the hierarchy of the seven major and
five minor notes disappeared and each of the twelve
notes carried equal value, which resulted in harsh,
screaming tones. This was atonal music, the music of
fear and the subconscious. It was not meant to enter-
tain the ear but to reach the inner world of man, his yet
unthought thoughts and intimate feelings.

The Russian Stravinsky chose a different path. In the
world of music he was the first to go back to primitive
forms and try to express some barbaric vital force – a
feature which started to appear in other fields of art in
those days. In 1910 he composed the *Firebird*, and in
1911 *Petrushka*. The rough and brutal force in the
music of both ballets consciously reached back to the
primitive in a genre which was renowned for its traditional refinement (or even over-refinement).

The starting point of the Hungarian Béla Bartók
was, again, entirely different. In 1905 he began to collect folk-music systematically. His aim, however, was
different from those of the romantic composers, who,
as he once said, used folk-music in their own works in
a 'false folksy manner' to enrich their tunes and
reinforce their national character. Hungarian folk-
music has Asian origins; its tonality is different from
the European; it lacks majors and minors and it is
based on a special system. When Bartók integrated
elements of this music in his own, he had to follow different rules of harmony and rhythm from the usual
ones. The music he created is tense, bitter and grievous.
Its tunes are broken and dissonant. Altogether they
express the general depression of contemporary
society. His single-act opera, *Bluebeard's Castle*,

which he composed in 1911, has a symbolic significance in this respect. The key that Judith asks for so
many times in the opera opens the door only to a room
of horrors.

The attack against the old ideals of beauty and harmony took place, as we can see, in literature, music,
and also in the revival of Russian theatre and the newly
born German and Russian film. The most triumphant
assault, however, was made in fine arts. A whole army
of Russian, German, Czech, Hungarian and
Rumanian painters and sculptors set themselves to
carry out the programme laid down in the Russian
Kandinsky's work (*Ober das Geistige in der Kunst*,
1910): 'The breach with the traditional idea of beauty
is necessary.' The pictures that the great pioneer
Kandinsky painted at the beginning of the century still
reflect the wild burning colours of expressionism, but
there are gradually fewer and fewer objects present in
them. In his two paintings, both entitled *All Saints'
Day*, the human and animal figures emerging from the
background are already more or less colour effects
only, and later the large-format paintings of the *Four
Seasons* are dominated by these colour effects exclusively. The path of this decorative abstraction led him to
the strict and puritan constructivist abstraction based
on geometrical simplicity.

The major ambition and accomplishment of new
painting was the destruction of form. And how many
different ways they found to achieve their aim.
Chagall, who came from the Jewish community of
Vityebsk in Russia, preserved form, but used it in an
arbitrary way. Reality, memories and dreams mingled
in a world of brilliant reds, deep blues, greens and

45

yellows on his canvases. In the paintings of the Czech Frantisek Kupka figures literally fall into pieces (for example, in his studies on his own painting, *Girl Playing with a Ball*, which he had made the previous year, in 1908). From that time on he became a painter of highly coloured circles and geometrical abstraction.

In the case of the Hungarian activists, Lajos Kassák and László Moholy-Nagy, seeking new ways in painting was most consciously connected with a revolt against the old pattern of society. As the artist's widow, Sybil Moholy-Nagy, who had known her husband's ideas and aims deeply, wrote later:

A truly revolutionary new system would differ in all aspects from the familiar old pattern. It would eliminate first of all cagelike houses in slums, dead museums that glorify a false world picture, hospitals run for profit . . . To translate the full scope of his protest into visual symbols, Moholy needed a tabula rasa, a cleansing of all symbolic connotations reminiscent of the social order he had rejected.[10]

The revolutionaries of art intended to create a tabula rasa indeed both in society and art. In this respect the Russian avant garde painters, the constructivists and supremists, went farthest. They consciously attempted to break with Europe, wiped out even colours after forms on the threshold of World War I. In 1913 Kazimir Malevitch, the son of a sugar-beet factory foreman in Kiev, painted black squares, red rhombuses and triangles on a white background. His revolutionary companion, the Hungarian contemporary artist Lajos Kassák, wrote the following about Malevitch's paintings:

As the world concept of Medieval Gothic, man's longing for God is expressed in the pointed arch and the crenellation carved with infinite tolerance and care, so the collective view of the world has found its artistic manifestation in the square shape which suggests stability, lacks hierarchy and stretches out far; in pure colours and unornamented planes. Aesthetic beauty and decoration are replaced by economy.

And Malevitch, following this path, reached the unbeatable extreme and painted his *White square in a white background*, the literal tabula rasa. (His fellow countryman, Rodchenko could only 'deepen' the subject with painting his *Black on black*.) Similar processes also took place in sculpture, where the 'statues' of the Russian Archipenko and Naum Gabo or the Romanian Constantin Brancusi became arrangements in space made of marble, metal or glass. Furthermore, they chose new materials and new forms in their rejection of traditional sculpture.

This type of painting and sculpture was already the total elimination of traditional art. These artists no longer wanted to fill museums or the palaces of rich patrons with their works. Revolutionising art, they wanted to become the artists of the revolution. 'The social achievements of 1917 had been accomplished in our art in 1914', said the Russian Tatlin after the revolution. And let me quote the authentic Sybil Moholy-Nagy again: 'When Béla Kun broke the hateful ties and declared a Hungarian Soviet, Moholy together with many of his generation saw in him the messiah of a new world. With the flaming enthusiasm of youth he offered himself, his art, and his willingness to teach, to the Communist regime.'[11]

With the same blazing enthusiasm the Russian constructivist painters undertook to design ordinary fabrics and posters for campaigns, as did the

47

Hungarian activists, Sándor Bortnyik and Béla Uitz. Chagall, Kandinsky and Malevitch, motivated by the same feelings, prepared street decorations for demonstrations.

'Art transforms us, and we transform our surroundings', said Lajos Kassák. The avant garde painters of the Central and Eastern European countries joined forces to transform society, the human environment and everyday life. What a bitter accident of history it is that the encounter between artistic and social revolution was only to be a short episode. It was, however, an important manifestation of social history even in this short period.

3 Different modes of social revolt after World War I

The semi-success or semi-failure of modernisation opened different means to ideological and cultural revolt in Central and Eastern Europe around the turn of the century. Following the unprecedented trauma of World War I revolt became social and political reality, and, in different forms and with different aims, spread all over the area. On the surface historical events seemed to be almost incomprehensible and chaotic. Revolutions and counter-revolutions followed one another; right-wing radicalist movements sprang up and attempted putsches took place; multi-national empires fell to pieces and new national states were born; previously non-existent states were created by the union of peoples, who were related across, but had previously been used to living within, the borders of separate countries. The territory of certain countries was reduced to one-third of the original, whereas others grew to three times their previous size. The map of Central and Eastern Europe was completely redrawn after World War I. Naturally, all these changes can be connected with the shock of the war, and in several countries with their being on the losing side. These large-scale historical changes, however, characterised the whole area: the victorious and the defeated were almost indiscriminately affected by social and national revolutions, counter-revolutions and right-wing radicalism. (As I have often pointed out before, the Southern European situation showed many similarities, so we could mention the Italian example as well.) It is interesting to note that, at the same time, the western half of the continent did not witness similar processes at all. This in itself can already imply that the reason for these sudden and chaotic changes did not simply lie in wartime ordeal, exhaustion and despair. The roots go much further down, to the pre-war historical development of the area, as shown above. And beneath the diversity and colourfulness of the apparently very confused historical events it is possible to find the common source from which the various modes of social and political revolt originated. In fact, there were three major kinds of transformation or attempts at alteration: (i) the revolutionary attempts of left-wing radicalism, of which the greatest and most successful was the 1917 Russian Bolshevik revolution. It was followed by the 133-day Hungarian and the even shorter Bavarian Soviet Republic and by the desperate revolutionary efforts of the German workers' movement during 1919–20. The reforms of government brought about by the socialists in Austria and by the democratic revolutionary peasant movement (led by Stambolisky) in Bulgaria, also followed this trend; (ii) national revolutions, which characterised mostly those countries that had lacked national independence previously or had been overshadowed by a huge empire which severely hindered their national development. These countries felt that all their economic, social and political ills were due to their dependence upon some powerful neighbour, and that the creation, re-establishment or significant enlargement and strengthening of an independent national state would provide a remedy for all their troubles. It was not by chance that this kind of revolt was the most common and most typical of the area from Czechoslovakia through Poland and Rumania to Yugoslavia and Albania; (iii) finally the right-wing radicalist attempt, which became obviously completely successful in the Southern European region only after World War I. Its first form of success was the triumph of fascism in Italy, which was, however, almost simultaneous with the attempted putsch of Hitler and Ludendorff. It appeared in a growing number of countries in various forms, sometimes in minority movements only, but its effects more and more often penetrated into the government. A new, dangerous shock, a great crisis was necessary for this trend to become dominant.

Although such a typological analysis is essential to our understanding of post-war processes, it must be emphasised at the same time that any such classification is a mere abstraction, since there were hardly any movements representing just one pure type; in most cases the different kinds of revolts mingled with each other. Right-wing radicalism often appeared in the guise of national revolution, but sometimes national revolutions, at least at the beginning, incorporated left-wing radicalist aims to cure social ills. At a later stage they often formed links with right-wing radicalist movements. Even those left-wing radicalist

51

attempts which were *par excellence* international could not help being connected with certain aims of the national revolutions of particular countries.

The mixing of the various movements, however, does not vitiate the endeavour to classify them in an abstract way. The two most significant examples of left-wing radicalism were the Russian and the Hungarian revolutions. The two showed many similarities. In both countries two revolutions followed one another within a short period. The events are well-known, and furthermore there is not space to give a detailed analysis of them within this book. What I should like to try to show, however, is where the events led to. In February, 1917, a huge demonstration took place in the streets of St Petersburg, when the police opened fire on the crowd. The militia, instead of helping the police in their attempt to control events, joined the demonstrators, turned against the Czarist government and, what is more, opened fire on the police who remained loyal to the government. This led to the fall of the Czarist government, the abdication of the Czar, the setting up of a temporary government and the achievement of democratic revolutionary changes. Following the example of the 1905 Russian revolution, workers', soldiers' and peasants' soviets were formed from the very beginning. A particular dualist power was created this way between the opposite poles of the central government and the soviets, which from April, 1917, made it possible for Lenin and the Bolsheviks to prepare a communist revolution. In October of the same year, given the historical circumstances, the Bolshevik revolution not only became triumphant, but also survived all the ordeals of the intervention and the civil war. The communist revolution succeeded in Russia, and from that time on the building of a new-type socio-political system could begin. The transformation into socialism had to do away with backwardness in the first place, and to form and carry out a programme of catching up.

Events in Hungary showed many structural similarities. In October, 1918, military units ordered to the front refused compliance and their revolt raised the democratic National Council to power. This soon led to the proclamation of the republic and to democratic changes. The democratic revolution led by Count Mihály Károlyi did not, however, last very long. (It is, in a way, an irony of history, but also very typical of the social hierarchy and traditions of Hungary, that the Hungarians still needed an aristocrat for the leadership of a democratic revolution.) The serious territorial demands made by the triumphant powers that were actually presented to the Hungarian government by the French general, Vix, had severe consequences. The democratic republic collapsed, and the Hungarian workers made a desperate attempt to create a new state: in March, 1919, they proclaimed the Hungarian proletarian dictatorship. The Hungarian Republic of Councils tried to alter the proprietorship and the socio-political system with remarkable speed, but after 133 days it collapsed before the intervention bearing down on the country from three directions. Rumanian troops even occupied Budapest in August. With the aid of the Czechoslovakians, the Rumanians and the French, the bloody counter-revolution led by Miklós Horthy prevailed in Hungary.

In Germany the left-wing workers' revolution did not achieve even temporary power. In November, 1918, though workers' and military councils were set up here too, the emperor abdicated and a social democratic government came into power. Moreover, because of the difference in conditions, the German socialist movement did not get to a stage of inner differentiation similar to the Russian or Hungarian. Naturally, there were different factions, but the majority, the Ebert–Noske wing wanted to follow the path of bourgeois democracy. A group of so-called independent socialists, les by Hasse, however, came up against the majority during the war and left the previously homogeneous movement. They represented a separate point of view in respect of the war only; their social and political programme did not go as far as the Bolshevik-type revolution. Only the Liebknecht–Luxemburg wing reached that stage, but they were supported by minor groups of workers only. Their revolutionary attempt in January, 1919, was condemned to death, and the sentence was carried out by the intact German army, the *Freikorps*, by order of the Eberg government. Liebknecht and Luxemburg were killed in 'attempted escape' and Berlin was reoccupied. On May 1, General Epp's troops subverted the Bavarian Republic of Councils too, which had lasted for about three weeks. The social democratic government of Germany aimed at forming a consistent bourgeois democratic system, and linked itself with the anti-revolutionary Prussian military forces. There was another revolutionary spasm in the Spring of 1921, but the general strike and the fierce fighting that went on in Hamburg, the Rhine-area and in other parts of

Germany for about a week were suppressed. And with this the revolutionary attempts of German workers came to an end.

The Bolshevik-type revolutionary movement in Austria was even weaker and even more hopeless. Although on February 1, 1918, the sailors hoisted the red flag in Cattaro, and in November there was a weak attempt at a take-over, there was hardly any real chance of success in Austria. 'Red Vienna' became dangerously isolated in the sea of conservative–Christian Austria, and it was not even supported by the social democrats because they were worried that the 'Bolshevik adventure' would spoil their chances of furthering democratic changes. Julius Deutsch, the military expert of the Austrian socialists, incorporated the Red Guards into the *Volkswehr*, and in 1919 a renewed revolutionary uprising was finally suppressed.

In Bulgaria, most people seeking for an answer to historical problems joined the left-wing opposition. In this backward agrarian country, where there was hardly any industry, one-quarter of the voters cast their votes almost unprecedentedly with the newly formed Communist party in the elections of August, 1919. However, there was no opportunity of achieving a Bolshevik-type solution, because in these elections the Stambolisky-led revolutionary democratic peasant party won with an overwhelming majority and took over the government by constitutional means. Their programme was democratic transformation, fulfilled through attempts at social equality. The latter included a redistribution of land to equalise the existing system, which involved approximately 6 per cent of the land.

Bulgarian agriculture had been based on peasant smallholdings anyway, and in the redistribution the relatively larger units were divided. However, this democratic revolutionary peasant radicalism could not last long: it was suppressed after four years in power by a counter-revolution. The putsch was planned by Professor Cancov and carried out by General Veltshev in June, 1923. The traditional majority government fell, and Stambolisky was arrested and handed over to Macedonian terrorists who first tortured the peasant leader horribly and then killed him. The communists, who could have mobilised significant masses in the Summer of 1923, regarded the counter-revolution as mere rivalry between the 'two wings of the bourgeoisie', and took a neutral position. A few months later, when they revised their point of view and tried to shake off the power of the counter-revolutionary dictatorship, it was too late. The revolt ended in a massacre, and the counter-revolutionary system settled permanently in Bulgaria.

The communist and left-wing revolutions or revolutionary attempts were all put down in Central and Eastern Europe, except in Soviet Russia. In some countries of the area, primarily in Hungary and Bulgaria, classical counter-revolutions restored the previous order. The achievements of the revolution were almost immediately overturned and the old proprietorship and political structure were re-established. In other cases, chiefly in Germany and Austria, the repression of revolutionary attempts was linked with a strong democratisation of the social democratic government. They fought against the revolutionary left-wing and the conservative counter-revolution simultaneously (in Germany they put down not only the revolts in 1919–21, but also the attempt at a counter-revolution, the Kapp putsch), and they represented the programme of Western-type democratisation. This process, however, was extremely contradictory. Even though the Weimar republic laid down the most democratic constitution in the history of democracy with the help of Professor Max Weber, this Weimar democracy remained rather fragile and had a certain Janus-faced character as well; namely, behind the political institution, there was the Prussian junker army left intact, which was a dangerously destabilising force from the point of view of democracy, almost a counter-revolution built into the system. The political significance of the army, its particular 'state within a state' role, had far graver consequences than the so often criticised clause 48 of the Weimar constitution which ensured exceptional rights to the President.

Several countries found means other than class-revolution to cure their economic, social and political problems. The major alternative to class-revolution for peoples who formed part of traditionally multi-national empires was the national revolution. Most nations of the area that had lacked independence before, that had been oppressed sometimes for several hundred years, sprang up now and formed new states. The population of the area was often mixed, so in some cases the minorities joined the main body of the nation in neighbouring countries, or peoples that were more or less related to each other and lived next door to one another joined to create a new and bigger 'national' state (which itself became practically multi-national in most cases). Late national revolutions restored the independent statehood of Poland, which had been part of three empires after three divisions. The Czech and Moravian areas had been part of the Habsburg empire for hundreds of years and could separate only now, and together with the Slovaks, who had traditionally been living within the borders of the Hungarian Kingdom, they created a new, previously non-existent state, Czechoslovakia. Croatia, which had been subject either to the Hungarian crown or to the Austro–Hungarian monarchy, became united with Serbia, with the areas annexed by the peace treaty, Bosnia and Herzegovina, the Macedonian areas and Slovenia formed a new state, Yugoslavia. Rumania was created from the two traditional Rumanian principalities and from Transylvania which was, along with Bessarabia and other areas, annexed to Rumania by French dictat (a deed reinforced by the accession proclamation of the Rumanian minority in Transylvania). Thus, the territory of Rumania grew from 138,000 to 304,000 square kilometres.

After the national revolutions, the regaining of independence and the growth of state borders in certain cases, the new countries were faced with several problems. They tried to follow the Western example more efficiently and also undertook to solve social injustice and to find remedies for the ills of capitalism. The new Czechoslovakian state under President Masaryk made efforts to link national revolution with a programme of social improvement. As Josef Korbel stated, quoting Masaryk:

Accepting the fact that the 'current capitalistic social system' was one-sided and that 'every one-sidedness must sooner or later come to an end', Masaryk . . . nevertheless, warned that in the process of creating socialism 'one must keep carefully in mind the special qualities of the individual and the nation'. We will socialize the country together with the socialists, and we do it gladly. The Russian bourgeoisie failed to understand this and was, therefore, swept away . . . mankind is, indeed, moving toward socialism.[12]

The Polish national revolution, however, showed different features. It is almost symbolic that the hero of the restoration of national independence, Josef Piłsudski, turned his back on the socialist movement and chose the path of national revolution instead of the class-revolution. The Polish socialist movement had already split and had set off in two different directions at the turn of the century. The revolutionary wing led by Luxemburg operated within the Czarist empire. They expected the rise of Polish society through a proletarian revolution, carried out in union with the Russian proletariat. Piłsudski's wing gave priority to the re-establishment of the independent Polish state, and for this World War I provided opportunities. While the conservative Dmowski hoped to restore Polish national independence by fighting on the Russian side against the Germans, Piłsudski hoped to achieve the same by fighting on the German side against the Russian Empire. In addition to the opportunity given by the war, the intervention which followed the Bolshevik revolution opened up new potentialities; it was in that war against Soviet Russia that the borders of the independent Polish state were confirmed in 1920. The social, and especially the socialist, aims were very vague at that time. A brief anecdote reflects Piłsudski's views very well: when he came into power and his ex-colleagues from the socialist party went to see him and greeted him as comrade, Pilsudski gave an immediate and unambiguous answer: 'Gentlemen, I am no longer your comrade. In the beginning we followed the same direction and took the same red-painted streetcar. As for me, I got off at "Independence" station. You are continuing the trip till you reach the "Socialism" stop. My best wishes accompany you, but . . . call me mister.'[13]

No special social programme was linked with the national one in the cases of the Yugoslavian and Rumanian national revolutions. In the euphoria after the end of the war and the national success, the leaders of these movements and the enthusiastic masses expected great achievements almost automatically from the reconstructed or strengthened national framework.

Analysing the late national revolutions that took place in the area, one has to draw attention to a most particular one: Zionism. Central and Eastern Europe had a vast population of Jews. They were spread all over the area, but in some places they formed closed units. In the Austro–Hungarian monarchy, except for Galicia, they were rapidly assimilated into the rest of the populatioon, but this was, however, less true in the Russian Empire and in the Polish and Rumanian areas. They lived in multi-national empires, but they were somewhat different from other minorities: in a way they were inferior and excluded partly because they were isolated by their own religion and traditions. They were, however, seeking ways to break out of this social exclusion. In some cases they chose the path

of rapid assimilation, which was, however, only possible in countries with more liberal governments.
Where they failed in their attempts to assimilate, they
turned to the socialist movement, which promised real
equality and internationality. This is why Jewish
workers and intellectuals rushed to join the communist
movement in Russia and in Hungary. This partly
explains why there were so many artists of Jewish
origin (from Kafka to Schoenberg; from Archipenko
to Marcel Jancu and Chagall) in the aforementioned
artistic revolution and why they were so sensitive to
changes in Central and Eastern Europe.

There was, however, another similarly natural
reaction – that of consciously facing the consequences
of their isolation and alienness. Sigmund Freud made a
witty remark about this when describing his Viennese
experiences in his autobiography: 'Above all, I found
that I was expected to feel myself inferior and an alien
because I was a Jew. I refused absolutely to do the first
of these things.'[14] This attitude was only a few steps
from creating a national programme based on this
isolated alienness and to the re-establishment of an
independent Jewish state which had been sunk in
thousands of years of history. It was hardly by mere
accident that Theodore Herzl, who had been born in
Budapest but lived in Vienna, drew up the political
programme of Zionism in the more backward zone of
Europe, amongst the late national revolutions of
Central and Eastern Europe. It was not by sheer chance
either that the first Jewish immigrants who went
to Palestine to start the preparations for the re-
establishment of the independent Jewish state came

from here, especially from the Russian and Polish areas. (Until World War I Palestine was under Turkish, and, after the war, under British authority.)

I mentioned previously that the different attempts to solve social contradictions and the various revolts often mingled together. One of these tendencies, however, needc closer examination: the tendency which gradually deformed national revolutions into more and more nationalistic revolts, and right-wing radicalism. It was, in fact, an almost general tendency which increasingly permeated the basically democratic national movements in most countries. Or, in other words, the national revolutions, in most cases, emerged from this trend deformed and oppressed as various kinds of right-wing dictatorship.

The most typical example of this process is Poland. The re-unification of the divided country and the repeated re-establishment of its independence was naturally in total accord with the international requirements of democratic bourgeois development. The newly born Polish Republic undertook all this consciously when it drew up and enacted its constitution according to the best democratic pattern. Later on, however, the Polish political system gradually became right-wing. During the period between the mid-1920s and mid-1930s three major phases could be observed. The first was the Pilsudski putsch and military take-over in 1926. The second phase started in 1930, already within the Pilsudski regime with the drastic winding up of the opposition and the notorious mass arrests. Finally, the third phase began after Pilsudski's death in 1935. Then the military (the Colonels') junta took over the government and introduced a new form of state, the dictatorship with no dictator. They tried to copy the Italian example of fascism, and in the meantime they became more and more right-wing oriented.

In Czechoslovakia and Yugoslavia the national revolutions generated new national movements almost immediately after the new states were set up. These movements had more and more extreme nationalist impulses and became the seed-bed of fascism. For example, the national movement that had created Czechoslovakia followed the same line only while they represented Czechoslovakian interests against the Austro–Hungarian monarchy; as soon as Czecho-slovakia came into existence, however, the Czech and Slovak interests separated. Hlinka and his followers attacked the Masaryk and Benes government more and more sharply. They accused them of violating the Pittsburg treaty which had proclaimed the Slovakian accession. Vojtech Tuka said outright that the Slovaks had not got those rights and autonomy that had been declared as the condition of the union in a secret clause of the agreement. Consequently, he said, the agree-ment was not lawful any longer, which created a *vacuum juris*. The national grievances and the demand for autonomy, linked with Catholicism, formed a basis for a Slovakian national movement. It gradually became more and more infused with fascism and sought the alliance of Nazi Germany against the Czechs. Eventually, after the annexation of Czecho-slovakia, an 'independent' fascist Slovak state came into being – with Hitler's assistance.

The tension between Serbs and Croats which emerged after Yugoslavia had come into being was very similar. Serbian centralism and Croatian separatism led to severe conflicts, with shooting in parliament and political terrorism in general. The Croatian national movement took up right-wing radicalism, and after the German occupation of Yugoslavia Croatia became an 'independent' fascist state led by Ante Pavelic.

Thus, the late national revolutions created new states, but all these states were ethnically heterogeneous. The multi-national character of these countries led to the 'fragmentation' of the national revolution: smaller and smaller national groups and minorities stood up, one after the other, demanding their own rights. During the period between the two world wars they all turned towards Italian fascism or perhaps even more to German Nazism to find their allies and they also adjusted themselves to a similar pattern.

The drift of the national revolutions towards the right did not take place in this form only. The new independent states or considerably enlarged countries expected to find remedies for all ills in the national euphoria following World War I. Very soon, however, they had to face the disillusioning reality: the success of the national revolution did not provide a panacea for social, political and economic backwardness, and the disappointment after such heightened expectations was particularly bitter. Its effect appeared after the great crisis. It seemed impossible that the social and economic tragedy, deepened by the crisis, could be cured with nationalist slogans. In most cases the answer was to link the national idea and aims with right-wing radicalism. They gave up former attempts at democratisation, often violated the parliamentary system, suspended parties, turned to mystical ideologies and set up dictatorships. These dictator-ships relied on social and national demagogy and borrowed uniforms and raising-of-the-arm greetings from the props room of fascism and Nazism. The so-called royal dictatorship of the Balkan countries fitted in to this pattern very smoothly: Yugoslavia, Bulgaria and Rumania created their own kind of totalitarian-ism. Though in different forms, similar tendencies were embodied in the strange catholic–Heimwehr fascism of Austria. Thus, the national revolutions drifted towards some form of right-wing radicalism with formidable regularity.

It is, however, worth drawing attention to the par-ticularity of the Hungarian situation, in which differ-ent tendencies and revolts strangely intermingled and which, at the same time, still led to an obvious shift towards right-wing radicalism. As I have mentioned, after the shock of World War I, Hungary was one of the Central European countries in which the long maturing revolt broke out in the form of a proletarian class-revolution, the Hungarian Republic of Councils; this revolution was thwarted with external help. After-wards the 'white terror' led by Miklós Horthy restored the previous regime in the form of a classical counter-revolution. At the same time, the new-born counter-revolutionary system appeared in the guise of national revolution. The reason was the Trianon peace treaty which had been signed and accepted by the country's representatives, but, however, gravely affronted the very principles of ethnic identity. Accordingly, the main target in the politics of the Horthy regime was territorial revision all through the period between the two world wars. Such aims turned Hungary against not only the neighbouring countries but also the triumphant great powers, and consequently isolated the country to an extreme. Following the logic of the situation, Hungary's hope of finding a way out and receiving help with its territorial demands against the neighbouring countries lay exclusively with the right-wing dictatorships which aimed at upsetting the peace treaty. This is how the political alliance was formed with Mussolini's Italy in the mid-1920s and later, after Hitler's take-over, with Germany as well. In such a framework, the original anticommunist, antiliberal and dictatorial character of the system mingled with Nazi–fascist elements, and even with attempts to introduce a German-type totalitarian system. Thus, the classical counter-revolution, while trying to perform its national role, became more and more interlinked with right-wing radicalist revolt.

However mixed the various forms of revolt were in the Central and Eastern European countries, however much they lost their original character, it is still possible and necessary to distinguish between them and to mark out the third type of revolt: pure right-wing radicalism. This varied and in itself colourful historical feature, which also grew out of the failure of modernisation, has built up a vast literature. One of the distinguished scholars of the subject, Eugen Weber, regards this 'fascist revolution' as a distinct type amongst the various possible kinds of revolution: 'We should abandon the notion of one revolution, identified with only one direction or theme and replace it with the question "what kind of revolution is it?" '[15]

66

Arguing against this view Arno Mayer uses the following witty terms: fascism, he says, is not an alternative revolution, but the alternative to revolution. It is not one of the possible revolutions, but a riposte contrary to and in place of revolution. This view seems to have had a strong influence on the way in which the Italian revolutionary anarchist, Fabri, saw it: he said that fascism was pre-emptive counter-revolution. In this sense it is a kind of revolt which turns towards some kind of right-wing radicalism in a sharpening revolutionary situation or simply in fear of a proletarian revolution. Hugh Trevor-Roper agrees with this when he says that fascism was born from fear, and even though it had had independent intellectual roots its strength and dynamism grew out of a new fear, the fear of the proletarian revolution.

This motive had already played an important role in the rise of the Nazi movement and the success of Italian fascism during the revolutionary period after World War I, but it gained particular significance during the great crisis; that is, the social and economic tragedy caused by the crisis foreshadowed a new revolutionary wave in the early 1930s and exaggerated its likelihood. It was only a decade after the revolutionary wave in Central and Eastern Europe when the Soviet Union and Hungarian and Bavarian Republics of Councils were born. On the one hand the ruling elite developed stronger self-protective reflexes, and on the other the numerous middle class demanded security against a proletarian revolution. Such a revolution would have meant their becoming declassed in a situation where their basic means of living were already threatened. But they also sought security against the pressure of traditional capitalistic competition and their own defencelessness; they wished to become an independent social factor in their own right; and they wanted 'order' and a firm-handed government. Thus, they ensured mass support for right-wing radicalism. 'The lower-middle class', N. Kogan wrote, 'rejecting proletarian egalitarianism as socially degrading, while not having a secure social position itself, would be most vulnerable to the fascist appeal.'[16] In other words, this 'pre-emptive counter-revolution' did not attempt to restore or maintain the previous regime, but proclaimed the necessity of radical changes itself. (Even though this social rhetoric did not really correspond to the political practice of the ruling fascism or Nazism.) These kinds of totalitarian dictatorship, however, meant a politically (and also in some respects economically) different model of capitalism from the liberal and industrialised Western democracies.

Eventually, given the historical situation of class-revolutionary attempts following World War I, the threat of the great crash and the 'hangover' after the euphoria of the national revolutions it became clear that the most powerful and most frequent form of revolt in Central and Eastern Europe was right-wing radicalism between the two world wars. (Here one has to draw attention to the similarity of the Southern European pattern, i.e. Italian fascism, Primo de Rivera, then Franco's Spanish and Salazar's Portuguese dictatorship.) In Germany Nazism came to power constitutionally; in Austria the Dollfuss–Schuschnigg regime took over; Rumania was dominated by the vast mass movement of 'popular' fascism; the Polish and Hungarian political systems drifted towards the right, towards fascism; in the Balkan countries royal dictatorships came into being. In most countries of the area parliamentary democracy was disregarded, single-party systems were introduced or 'national fronts' emerged with dictatorial, hyper-national and extremely anticommunist programmes. These regimes promised a new-type modernisation, but, as John Weiss rightly points out, the reality differed radically from the promises they had made in their slogans before their take-over. It is also well-known with what ruthless brutality they slaughtered even their own supporters who took the 'socialist' side of national socialism seriously after the take-over. They finished off any attempts at social reform within the movement either by purging the party of its own left-wing, or by 'nationalising' the fascist or Nazi parties or simply by force ('the night of long knives'). However, Nazism and fascism became really strong and dangerous by making the best use of social revolutionary forces. In Italy this was institutionalised mainly through the corporate system, while Hitler relied on his anti-Semitic programme. As G. Mosse rightly states:

The German revolution became the anti-Jewish revolution . . . Here then was the source of Hitler's success: his ability to transform the populace into anti-Jewish revolution. Not the big capitalist or the economic middleman, but the Jew, was made the incarnation of the enemy. In his deft and ingenious distinction between Jewish and German capitalism, Hitler saved the capitalist structure of Germany.[17]

The Rumanian Iron Guard and the Hitler-following Hungarian 'arrow-cross' movement received their strength from the same above-mentioned source. The latter, the Hungarian Nazi movement, became so successful that it gained one-quarter of the votes in the 1939 election.

As has been described previously, the modernisation that had taken place in the Central and Eastern European countries was ambiguous and only partially successful. Economically, socially and politically they remained on the periphery; consequently, they had lacked the opportunity to build empires and become great powers. These unfulfilled desires and ambitions led to frustration and created the feeling of backwardness. All this was good ground for the bitter revolts that emerged with various aims and social bases between the two world wars. Even though this historical feature was the result of semi-success, semi-failure of modernisation, the peripheral status of these countries (peripheral in the broadest sense, not only in economic terms), it must be noted that revolts and radicalism with similar significance in ideology and mass movements also appeared in rich, developed and socially modernised countries whose national development had not been obstructed and which had even been successful in creating empires. Pre-fascist ideologies had spread all over France after the defeat the country suffered from Germany at the end of the nineteenth century, and by the 1930s and 1940s the fascist movement represented a significant force in France. These ideologies sprang up in England, Belgium, Holland and the United States, too. These developed capitalist systems also provoked their left-wing antithesis: the socialist movement. After World War I communist parties were formed. These countries also witnessed revolts and disillusionment as a result of the contradictions and halts in capitalist development around the turn of the century and, later, between the two world wars, due to the slow-down of development and to the severe economic and social crisis. However, the various revolts did not prevail in the rich centre of the world. As Eugen Weber neatly puts it: 'the consumer state consumes its revolution, too.'

4 The arts in the period of crisis and fascism: the art of resistance

The great crisis raised again the question posed previously by the failures of modernisation. However, since the once defeated and divided forces of class-revolution could not offer a real alternative, and since even the national revolutions themselves mingled more and more with right-wing radicalism from the 1930s, most of the Central and Eastern European countries were irresistibly drifting towards the extreme right. And since actual mass movements contributed to this process, the large-scale movement to the right permeated the cultural sphere of social activity as well, as was the case in the earlier spiritual preparation for left-wing revolutions. As the revolution of art became the art of the revolution after the turn of the century and around World War I, so did the art of the crisis cause the crisis of art in the 1930s. These processes would have been unimaginable without a counter-revolution of popular art, just like Nazism and fascism which could not exist without a mass movement. The artistic revolt of the avant garde called forth this artistic response as a matter of course. Contrary to the avant garde which destroyed colour and shape and gave way to functionalism and mass production, the new tendency turned back to classicism, often to naturalistic representation of the world and traditional artistic forms. Berthold Hinz analyses this counter-revolution of art in his book *Art in the Third Reich* very well: he describes how powerfully this movement sprang up and directed itself against the avant garde. Nazism created an opportunity for thousands of artists who followed the traditional, old-fashioned trends, who had stood out against modernism and been left behind on the peripheries of art. Tens of thousands of German artists joined the Nazi movement for this very reason years before Hitler's coming to power. In 1930 there were no fewer than a quarter of a million members of the Nazi Leaders' Council of Cultural and Art Societies! How eager they were to follow Hitler and to finish with the modernism that had swept them aside. This *Führerrat* of Nazi artists issued its manifesto entitled *What German artists expect from the New Government* in the *Deutscher Kunstbericht* (German Art Report) only a month after Hitler's take-over. It said:

... there will be only *one* guideline for action from now on, and that guideline is a philosophy drawn from a passionate national and state consciousness anchored in the realities of blood and history! . . . Bolshevist non-art and non-culture will be doomed to destruction . . . They must give way to the scores of artists loyal to the German tradition. The conscious care and nurturing of all existing impulses . . . will have to go hand in hand with the radical negation that will free us from the nightmare of the past years! Our powers are waiting to be called to life! The people's love for art, immobilized by the terror of artistic Bolshevism, will reawaken.[18]

The mass power of this artistic counter-revolution is well illustrated by the fact that, as Hinz rightly states:

'thousands of artists sent thousands of works to the official art exhibitions held in the Third Reich. Art works in such vast numbers could not simply be willed into being. They must have already existed somewhere in some form.'[19] Undoubtedly, the fact that no fewer than 15,000 works arrived for the first representative art exhibition organised by the Nazis is really shocking. These works had obviously not been made by government order. From all this, Hinz draws the conclusion that the Nazi Government did not have to do anything but support the counter-revolution of third-class artists:

It is true that a noticeable change took place on the cultural scene; what appeared there, however, was not something new but something old, indeed, something antiquated. The claim that German fascism created its own art, and particularly its own painting, out of nothing can no longer be taken seriously. All it did was reactivate those artists who had been left behind by the development of modern art but who were still active after 1933 and who seized the opportunity to move into the vacuum once modern art had been liquidated.[19]

However, there was more to it than that, or rather it was slightly different. As in politics it was not the revolt of the petit bourgeois that created Nazism and fascism (they only guaranteed its mass force), nor was Nazi art the spontaneous product of mediocrity. The totalitarian regime wished to harness the arts to the carriage of its own political aims. The Nazi party and all kinds of fascist movements had a conscious art policy which originated in their ideology and its practice. On May 10, 1933, Goebbels announced in the *Völkischer Beobachter* that it was his Ministry's task to put Germany into a state of spiritual mobilisation: 'the Ministry has thus the same function in the area of spiritual matters as the War Ministry has in the field of armaments.'[20]

The accuracy of Goebbels' announcement can hardly be regarded as exaggerated. In addition to a spiritual mobilisation, however, there was also an attempt to standardise spiritual matters as well as taste. The well-known Nazi slogan was somewhat twisted: one nation, one Führer, one taste.

Nevertheless, however conscious an art policy and pre-planned programme the Nazi movement had, it is indisputable that the coincidence of events also contributed largely to the development of Nazi art. Such a coincidence was that Hitler himself was an unsuccessful, mediocre painter who devoted a lot of energy to the indirect realisation of his imperfect, unmaterialised and even humiliated artistic ambitions. From the memoirs of Alfred Speer it is well-known how paternalistically he nurtured the talented young artist, thus fulfilling his own thwarted ambitions.

Similarly, the different artistic tastes of the two wings of the Nazi party was also a coincidence, as was the prevalence of the artistic conception which was born from the struggle between the two wings. Goebbels represented a more modern artistic taste than the several thousand members of the Nazi Art Association. This must have been due partly to the fact that he had had leanings towards the Marxist workers' movement before he joined Hitler, and even then at the beginning he was close to the Nazi 'left-wing' led by the Strasser brothers. In the party's internal disputes Goebbels first argued that the modern German expressionism should be announced as the official artistic trend, or at least it should be accepted as part of German and national socialist art. In his view the art of Nolde and Barlach could have been an integral part of Nazi art, instead of which their art was considered unacceptable and was banned by the *Füherrat* of Nazi art.

In contrast to Goebbels, Alfred Rosenberg represented the *Völkisch* right-wing of the Nazi party and professed extreme antimodernism and *Völkisch* traditionalism. He could not accept expressionism, and in his view Emil Nolde, who had joined the Nazi party earlier, could not have a place in the national socialist art of Germany. In these internal debates the scales were tipped by the Führer who was interested in art anyway, and regarded himself as an authority. In this case he decided in favour of Rosenberg almost immediately, and Goebbels, who had turned his back on the Strasser brothers in time, accepted Hitler's opinion without reservation. Already in 1930, during a debate with Otto Strasser who was leaving the party then, Hitler made his point of view unmistakably clear: 'There is no such thing as a Revolution in art: there is only one eternal art – the Greek–Nordic art . . . and anything which deserves the name of art can always be only Nordic–Greek.'[21] Hitler left no doubt whatever about the realisation of this view after he had come to power. On March 23, 1933, in the manifesto speech which he gave in the Reichstag about the tasks of the new government, he proclaimed the demand for moral as well as political cleansing. Education, the press, films, theatre and literature, he said, must serve eternal values, and must clearly express the German character.

Nazi art policy was to maintain the cult of German greatness and heroism, the clearness of species and blood, and the beauty of health and strength.

Nazi totalitarianism was executed with the usual German thoroughness and perfectionism. Thus, they not only wanted to give the new works of art a character which would correspond to their aims, but they also found it essential to destroy those works which did not match their theory. They set up a committee led by Professor Adolf Ziegler, a third-class painter of rigid, naked women, with exactly this purpose: they confiscated and collected 16,000 paintings and statues of 1400 artists from German museums (among them more than 1000 paintings of Nolde). They organised an exhibition of these works in 1937 which was meant to be a warning (*Entartete Kunst*) and demonstration of the nihilism, deformity and idiocy of Bolshevik non-art. This 'warning' exhibition intended to make the restrictions absolutely clear, and as a further threat they burnt or broke approximately 4000 pictures and statues in the central courtyard of the Berlin Fire-brigade on March 20, 1939. The fate of books incompatible with the Nazi spirit was similar: they were also set on fire and their light was a beacon for the course laid down by Nazi art policy. (How fortunate it was that some of the confiscated works were sold for hard currency abroad.)

Almost parallel to this warning exhibition they organised a representative exhibition of 'healthy' German art to demonstrate a positive example. The exhibited material, which was carefully selected with Hitler's personal contribution, gave an accurate inventory of the iconographic regulations of Nazi art.

77

Perhaps surprisingly at first sight, 40 per cent of the paintings were naturalistic landscapes. Landscape, as such, was supposed to carry a particular ideological significance; as Dr Kauffman interpreted new German painting in his book in 1941: 'Where there is so much feeling for the soil in which we are rooted, the pure landscape is bound to be an object of artistic interest ... These landscapes are *representations of the fatherland* ... Sometimes, it is a piece of the Reich that demands our loyalty.'[22] Another 16 per cent of the paintings ventured to express masculine strength and female duty. These pictures were inhabited by fighting soldiers and hard-working peasants and workers who supplied the soldiers with food and weapons, and healthy women determined to conceive and bear future soldiers. Thus nakedness represented coldly, without eroticism or sexuality, gained a particular patriotic and national socialist significance. Let us quote the interpretation of the authoritative Dr Kauffman again:

In nudes, the artist tries to show the healthy physical being, the biological value of the individual as a precondition of all popular and spiritual rebirth. He concentrates on the body as nature wanted it, on perfect forms ... on a modern and therefore palpably athletic classical ideal ... Our country is particularly intent on cultivating such happiness where it promises to enhance the performance of men and women in their basic duties of combat and fertility.[23]

A whole collection of the above-mentioned iconographical elements appears in R. Heymann's painting, *In Good Hands*: the landscape, motherhood and a lot of children. In Schmitz-Wiedenbrück's painting *Workers, peasants, soldiers* the three services are represented: the German soldiers were placed in the middle with miners on one side and a peasant leading a cow on the other. The composition followed the classical triptych form of altarpieces, and the intellectual content was propagated in a rather didactic form.

Otherwise a further 12 per cent of the paintings in this representative exhibition pictured labouring workers, peasants cultivating the land and soldiers stiffened into a heroic pose. A further 1.5 per cent of the paintings were devoted to the Führer. In these paintings the Führer often appeared as a romantic, solitary hero. In Georg Poppe's painting, *The Führer at the Medical Association in Frankfurt*, however, he was pictured among soldiers and white-coated doctors. There was also a mother holding a small child, looking at the Führer with devotion, a workers' brigade, with the swastika, carrying shovels, a motorway under construction, aeroplanes flying high in the sky, a peasant woman and a girl holding flowers at the side of the painting, etc. The direct propaganda aim of the work was combined with a compulsory national socialist naturalism.

Hitler's favourite and official sculptor was Josef Thorak. The Führer gave him a huge, 51 foot high studio, and he often visited him there unexpectedly to get away from the cares of government. There he would put his hand on the artist's shoulder, and, while walking, he would talk about art with him. Josef Thorak made huge, classicist statues with robust strength. Some of these statues decorated the new Chancellor's palace, which was a product of Nazi art with cult significance. The Chancellor's palace, which was built by the brilliant organiser, Albert Speer, in just one year, was the manifestation of greatness and strength, power and order and everlasting existence with its eternal classicism and gigantic size. From the memoirs of Albert Speer one can learn how conscious the intention in Nazi art was to create always something great or even gigantic, and also what motivated the artists. Hitler's intentions were, according to Speer, the following: 'On the long walk from the entrance to the reception hall, they'll get a taste of the power and grandeur of the German Reich!'[24] There was even a psychological element revealed in Hitler's words, with which Speer explained the significance and function of monumentality: 'Why always the biggest? I do this to restore to each individual German his self-respect. In a hundred areas I want to say to the individual: We are not inferior; the very opposite.'[25]

This psychological feature can be regarded as an over-compensated inferiority complex of a pathological personality. It may, however, have a symbolic aspect too: not only the failed individual but also those nations which consider themselves unsuccessful wish to prove their own greatness and strength again and again. This is why rigid monumentality, classical eternity and the heroic pose became the demand and the characteristic feature of fascist or similar-to-fascist dictatorial regimes in most of Central and Eastern Europe. In this case, therefore, I do not share Hinz's view, whose work I have so strongly relied on previously. He denies the possibility and importance of generalisation and says that one cannot trace a relationship between the art of Italian fascism or other dictatorships and the art of Nazism. It is indisputable that there are differences, and in some cases they are not at all insignificant. No doubt the art of Italian fascism, the *novocento*, preserved more of modernism than Nazi art which sank back towards eighteenth century naturalistic genre painting. The remains of futurism, which Hitler banned and condemned, can still be found in the Italian *novocento*. (This must have been partly due to the fact that the Italian futurists and their leader Marinetti took the side of fascism from the beginning; moreover, Marinetti belonged to Mussolini's personal circle.) The Italian *novocento*, when reaching back into the past to find traditions for fascist art, chose the *trecento* 'primitivism' to be its predecessor, while Nazi art chose naturalism and empty classicism.

Even though this was a considerable difference, the heroic pose, the empty exaggeration, the artificial monumentality and the classicism of the ancient Roman references, aimed at increasing self-respect, were only too similar.

The similarities and differences which connected the Italian fascist *novocento* with Nazi art made this trend particularly attractive to the Central and Eastern European countries, whose dictatorships were keen on following the spirit of contemporary art, but found *novocento* more acceptable and easier to follow than the aggressive, frightening and depressing Nazi art of Germany. The greater effect and attraction of *novocento* in art policy can hardly be studied separately from those political motives that influenced Horthy, Stojadinović and others to seek alliance with Mussolini, thus trying to find a guarantee against the danger of an alliance with Germany.

Of all the countries of the area, Hungary was,

perhaps, the most consciously connected with the art of the Italian fascist *novocento*. A comprehensive grant system was created to provide for the carefully selected young talents, who were sent to Rome by the government to learn and follow not so much the past but the present artistic trends. Vilmos Aba-Novák, C. Pál Molnár, Pál Pátzay and many others went to this Rome school and introduced a special *novocento*-type mixture of modernism and classicism at home. In Hungary, particularly from the late 1930s the historical and religious subjects, the sentimental representation of national heroes and saints, and the huge frescoes of Aba-Novák became, perhaps, the highest quality contemporary manifestations of artistic form and content in the area.

It is also to be noted that the *novocento* trend was all the more followable in most Central and Eastern European countries because its form and message were closely connected with the ideology of the late national revolutions in some countries. It mingled with the efforts to create a historical identity and with the typically romantic nineteenth century artistic expressions of these efforts. The similarities are fairly strong. This is how the historical romantic painting of the Bulgarian Rukarov of the heroic national fights became related to the frescoes of Aba-Novák of around 1938 and to the Italian *novocento*.

Naturally, this was closely linked with the artistic reaction which emerged against turn of the century avant garde almost everywhere, and which, independently of the fascist artistic trends, showed a return towards classicism even in the progressive trends.

Forms and colours were universally re-established in

painting, and so was the hexameter in poetry. There were many elements in it. One of the reasons was, perhaps, the emerging crisis of avant garde itself. The crisis had two aspects: the exhaustion of the artistic trend and its commercialisation. It is true, though, that after World War I it seemed as if avant garde was having a colourful rejuvenation in Central and Eastern Europe; moreover, some of these backward countries only became really acquainted with the novelties of the 1910s at that time. The Polish, Rumanian, Yugoslavian and Czechoslovakian avant garde flourished rapidly one after the other, mixing the different trends which had emerged in the meantime. Significant achievements were made by varius groups or individual artists of the avant garde, e.g. the circle of the Rumanian *Contimporanul* periodical; the 'Integral' group which aimed at some kind of modernist synthesis as its name also suggests; the Polish *Nowa Sztuka* or the *Blok* group; the Yugoslavian *Zenit* movement, the Czech *Devetsil*, or the Hungarians Lajos Kassák, László Moholy-Nagy and Marcell Breuer who worked in exile after the defeat of the revolution. Still, this post-revolutionary avant garde seemed somewhat different from the pre-revolutionary movement. Then it had been part of the preparation for social changes; now, following the disappointment and disillusionment, it turned away from society and kept only a defiant utopianism. This soon led to the lack of serious message and the growing significance of the empty form. The greatest social value of avant garde used to lie in its conscious social action and reaction, but now all it retained was an increasingly self-repeating game of colours and forms. A

Hungarian art critic, György Bálint, who had come from the avant garde group, said that if avant garde artists had launched an attack against the 'ivory-tower' of art earlier, now they had built up their own ugly, reinforced concrete towers.

Another important revolutionary innovation of the avant garde was its widespread functionalism which served the masses. This functionalism dominated in the design of homes for the everyday man, of furniture, textiles, household goods, books, etc. The trend reached its peak in the activity of the Bauhaus in Germany after World War I, but it also soon reached deadlock. The Bauhaus, led by the German pioneer of modern functionalist architecture, Walter Gropius, became an international artistic centre of Central and Eastern Europe where Germans, Russians and Hungarians were united in the attempt to create an art which served mankind. This artistic movement was meant in a way to fulfil what the early philosophy of the avant garde aimed at, but could not achieve: to change society. However, these functionally as well as artistically designed houses and objects soon became commercialised, since they fell prey to those entrepreneurs who saw great profit in the innovations. The Hungarian Marcell Breuer designed and constructed the first modern tubular furniture, a manifestation of modern functional art and avant garde philosophy, which, however, became the mass product of an English furniture factory. Thus, modern design gradually left the sphere of arts and became part of industrial mass-production.

Despite the exhaustion and commercialisation, avant garde did have another new offshoot, and not just an ordinary one. This new offshoot was surrealism which emerged in the mid-1920s and professed the joint liberation of society and the individual. Its exponents pinned the names of Marx and Freud on their banners: they aimed at social liberation in Marxist terms, and for this they considered the liberation of the individual in the Freudian spirit essential. Following Freud, the surrealist artists went further; they wanted to conquer the land of the irrational, too. Despite the fact that this trend also had strong roots in Central and Eastern Europe, the movement itself did not originate in the area so much as earlier trends of the avant garde. A great many works of art of the period were, however, conceived in close connection with this trend. The Czech Josef Sima, the Rumanian Victor Brauner, the Hungarian Lajos Vajda and a lot of others expressed their humanist message in the spirit of surrealism, and warned against the dangers and depression threatening the area and mankind in general.

The progressive attempts of surrealism, however, were rather isolated in Central and Eastern Europe. As social reaction became more and more depressing and as right-wing radicalism became more and more dominant and threatening, the defence of social and human values demanded such artistic action such as could pass on the message to the masses in the most direct and obvious way, which could reveal disorder and mobilise people, and which could become true social action and resistance.

In most countries of the analysed area conditions for political resistance were more and more severe due to the growing power of the right-wing dictatorships, particularly from the 1930s. Since the major strength of right-wing movements lay in the fact that they could take the wind of discontent and revolution in their own sails, joining right-wing movements and collaborating with right-wing regimes was widespread. Thus, resistance in the artistic field became a major kind of social resistance, a defensive action. This led, as a matter of course, to certain trends which preserved many of the important achievements of the modernists, but which still turned towards realism and were called 'neo-realist' in several countries. This is how the documentarist trend developed with great strength, not independently of the universal artistic movement. This *par excellence* realist genre appeared in various fields of art. The misery of the great crisis (the Wall Street Crash), and the growing threat of war, fear and humiliation were expressed with staggering force in the sociographical works of the Slovakian and Rumanian artists. They protested against the terrorist regimes, misery and starvation, and they had a moving effect. Similar features characterised the Czechoslovakian and – at the very beginning of the 1930s – the German film art which expressed its protest by showing the everyday life of the street, the city and the unemployed using the simplest possible means. Thus did another outstanding achievement of documentarism, the Hungarian sociographical literature, emerge in the 1930s. A new group of writers who had risen from among the peasantry started to study the Hungarian village. Their description of the misery, the defencelessness and humiliation of the Hungarian peasant was indeed shocking.

Besides the directly political and protesting

documentarism, another literary genre developed which reached a particularly high artistic level: the literature of the grotesque. It was another form for preserving the traditional human and social values of protesting against spreading irrationalism and darkness. The Croatian Miloslav Krleža started to write and publish his huge protest entitled *Banquette in Blitva* in which he scourged history through an imaginary country, Blitva. He constructed Blitva from the distorted features of all the Central and Eastern European countries. Karel Čapek also turned towards the means of the grotesque to rouse and warn against the aggression and the growing dangers of Nazism. A Polish representative of the genre, Gombrovicz, started his literary career at the same time, and wrote some of the greatest classics of the time.

The protest and the effort to preserve traditional values had, however, a further kind of artistic manifestation which was quieter and more resigned than the others, but was not in the least weaker in its artistic expression. It was briefly called 'catastrophism', expressing the essence of the genre. The contents, in this case, dominated over the form.

Several representatives of the Rumanian, Slovakian or Hungarian surrealism had already expressed the message of catastrophism. The Hungarian Lajos Vajda, in the last years of his short life, populated his canvasses with imaginary creatures, horrifying black-winged spectres, and filled them with a depressing feeling of doom. This end-of-the-world atmosphere characterised the works of several artists who wanted to reveal and show the subconscious as well as the conscious sphere of the human mind. Rightly did the

Czech Nezval state, as early as 1931, when he commented on the Styrsky and Toyen exhibition, the following: 'This art demonstrates and at the same time negates the sharp contradictions prevailing in the unacceptably bad social-economic order of the age, an order facing impending catastrophe.'

In the 1930s the presentation of an impending 'universal catastrophe' pervaded and manifested itself in East-Central European art in the most varied forms and ways.

Catastrophism, even though it cannot be regarded as an 'ism' of a uniform idiom similar to any other artistic trend, did determine content and universal message. As the approach of the universal catastrophe became more and more evident with the advance of time, the alarm and even the feeling of being condemned to death grew stronger and stronger.

In his poem entitled *May Day* (1932) V. Zavada, son of an Ostrava mining family, a poet who joined the avant garde camp, still expressed the desire 'to furnish the world like a clean room'. He still spoke about sweetly smelling flowers, pollen-carrying, wonder-working winds of the first of May, when the anguish of recognition cut short his imagination: 'Suddenly it looks to me', he wrote, 'as if a corpse were lying nearby under the lawn of the park.' The association of ideas characteristic of the Hungarian poet Attila József is very similar. In his poem in 1937, entitled *The Poet and his Age*, which begins in a light, playful tone, the author fancies that he sees blood and livid spots in the landscape at nightfall:

> Leave this and that, look at the light
> of the evening disperse with night

Red blood stains the stubble
And under the gentle slope lies
It clots in blue
The feeble
tiny grass droops and cries
Gently scattered livid spots
on the peaceful, glad hillocks
And the day slowly dies.

Halas published a book entitled *The Cock Scaring Death* (1930). In his *Old Woman*, written in 1936 to declare his programme, he describes with impersonal objectivity the transitoriness of life and the devastating work of death. The poem already represents the true attitude of the generation of the 1930s whose writings are imbued with the new spirit and world in a natural manner. The Czech V. Holan, the Bulgarian A. Balchev, the Pole C. Milos, or the Polish-Ukrainian I. Antanich have produced outstanding poems along these lines.

Let me mention here the obstinate certitude with which the Hungarian Miklos Radnoti acquiesces to the inevitability of death in his poem from 1936. The conscious knowledge of death, the death motif, recurs in his poems and escorts him everywhere; even a pleasant garden or the humming of bees remind him of it:

Oh, this garden, too slowly sleeps and dies
Unloading before the fall the harvest of the fruit-tree
Night is falling – and around me flies
in deadly circles a belated fair bee
And for you young men? What kind of death?
A bullet flying with a beetle-like sound
Or a noisy bomb exploding on earth
and with your flesh torn you will lie scattered around.

The contemporary critic of those poets was right in

claiming that it was not a matter of panic of death but simply 'of a consciousness of death'. It appears in the world of objects, sounds and plants in the complete harmony of reality and illusion.

> We have been condemned to death [wrote George Bálint] and, although we have been granted some time of grace, and will, naturally continue to live through it the best we can, thinking even of the future from time to time, evidently it will not be our future even if it is bound to come: 'There will be frost with snow to follow' but then 'one day at dawn the new grass will stick out its daggers'. So let us walk as long as we can. It will not be long but let it not damp our spirits . . . The shorter the time left, the more worthwhile it is to use it.[26]

The authenticity of these lines is reinforced a thousand-fold by the fact that they were written by a poet, Radnóti, and a critic, Bálint, who – as we were to learn subsequently – had actually been 'sentenced' to death. Both were only granted some delay but the verdict was finally carried out eight years later. The awareness of death did not change the human and artistic integrity of the best representatives of catastrophism. They tried to use the 'respite' for action. Let me quote here again Radnóti, who gave the following tragic picture of the world he lived in:

> I write and live deep in this
> crazy world like
> that oak lives there, knowing the coming death.
> Though the white
> cross shines on its bark – the woodcutter's sign
> who will come
> tomorrow and cut down the trees
> the oak waits for him
> but until tomorrow: still grows new leaves.

The arts in the period of crisis and fascism

The various trends at the beginning of the century shared a basic aim: they wanted to arouse protest and preserve real human and social values. This was present in the documentarist trend which wanted to show rough reality; in catastrophism which expressed a sense of death; in the art of the resistance which stood up against increasing fascism; in the latest avant garde trend; in surrealism; or in the most traditional realism; or occasionally in a particular synthesis of avant garde and realism.

In most branches of art a brave and progressive message appeared in new and traditional form simultaneously. However, the tendency to turn back towards the traditional became more and more common, which often meant a declaration of adherence to eternal human values in itself.

Content, social message and artistic–aesthetic form were combined, in my opinion, in the most homogeneous way in music. Music followed the same path from the beginning of the century most consistently; however, it did not dully repeat itself but went further and further in the achievement of modern art.

The music whose dissonant chords brayed the coming of catastrophe in the 1910s, however, was of course not free of self-repetition in the decades to come, nor of speculative experiments ending in empty formal experimentation.

The Czech Alois Haba attempted to dissect Schoenberg's twelve-tone system and experimented with a special scale of one-quarter and one-fifth tones instead of full tones. This could become neither reality nor music, just as the newer almost extreme experiments of the father of the school, Arnold Schoenberg, had to fail. Actually, the master consistently continued his attacks on beauty in the old sense. A decisive battle in this war was to be his opera *Moses and Aaron*, composed between 1926 and 1932. The conflict between the brothers was conceived as the clash of Truth and Beauty, of the Ideal and Life. With grim irony, Schoenberg composed the only opera in music history whose hero, Moses, impersonating Truth and the Ideal, is incapable of singing and only speaks, is too pure for art, and cannot reach Man – his song breaks out only in the brief erupting moments of final frustration, in the realisation of the failure of the Word.

Yet, from the Schoenberg School sprouted buds of unusual force, and the Schoenberg system inspired music created by his disciples more musical than his own theoretical, experimental works.

Alban Berg and Anton Webern were prominent representatives of the school. Berg, who died at 50 in 1935, left few but seminal works. Without his two operas, *Wozzek* and *Lulu*, no discussion of twentieth century music could be complete. It is exactly through Berg that Schoenberg's twelve-note system became simplified in structure and tone, losing its ascetic character and revealing its modern lyric drama, aided by a symbolic story and text. (To cite E. Lockspeiser's witticism: the Schoenberg student Alban Berg is the true schön-Berg!)

While Berg filled the new structure with living lyricism and dramatic force, Anton Webern also expanded on the method: with musical concepts set in one–two measure, with quickly changing tone colour and tone sequence, he achieved an unusual consciousness which culminated in his *Orchestral Variations*

Op. 30. The theme of this work consists of two and one-third measures of eight tones which are expressed in six variations. Webern's technique of consciousness and brevity already points to the musical experiments of the following age.

As in the beginning of the century Schoenberg, Stravinsky and Bartók had been a trio of trailblazers of a new music; they now with Berg and Webern formed a quintet which rearranged the music of the twentieth century.

The two younger composers could not, however, obscure the significance of the further artistic activities of the three original innovators. This, perhaps, applied also to the strangest member of the great trio, whose character and temperament was so different, yet equally inspiring: Igor Stravinsky took the least consistent path and was the most open to change.

Around 1920, when Stravinsky's music had passed through a period of pagan–primeval forcefulness, it suddenly changed to the neo-classicism which was appearing as a characteristic tendency of various branches of art at this time. 'Stravinsky's remark', notes Hans Hollander, 'that the Russian folklorism of his early works was a stylistic exercise, rather than the expression of some inner compulsion, put his further development in a noteworthy light.'[27]

His works turning to classicism in the 1920s exhibit an unusually pure and elevated intonation: his *Concertino*, his violin and piano concertos, his opera *Oedipus Rex* (from the text of the great art-lover J. Cocteau), his ballet *Apollon Musagetes* (stylised and objective in its intonation and at times reaching back to eighteenth century dance traditions), and especially his

Symphony of Psalms composed in 1930 (in spite of, or maybe because of, its religious theme, its Latin text, its at times conscious musical monotony and rigidity). Stravinsky, in turning to classical traditions and a cool and rational form of composition, uniquely combined in his new music the traditional with his inexhaustible flair for innovation. His old inspiration merged with his new ideas to become the source of ingenuity.

In contrast to Schoenberg, who did not deviate from the path he set out on, and to Stravinsky, who was consciously prepared to find new directions, was Béla Bartók, who had embarked and made progress on a path of his own. One of the period's greatest musical œuvres was built with a rare combination of genuine scholarly and artistic accomplishment.

Early on, Bartók had begun to collect and adapt folk-music which was to become his life's work and formed the basis of his entire musical concept. The primitive naturalness of Hungarian, Rumanian, Slovak and other folk-music he distilled through his intellect. Bartók saw folk-music not as something primeval and primitive – it did not lead him to methodical collection inspired by documentarism. Based on the musical systems developed around World War I and realised with increasing maturity, he created the exceptional synthesis which naturally melted pure folk-music with the epoch's most modern musical language. Primeval instincts joined intellectual social thinking and the ancient colloquial mixed with the modern urban vernacular. This all-embracing synthesis I find virtually unique in the art of the time. His mature great works of the 1930s: his *Cantata Profana* (1930); his *Music for Strings, Percussion and*

Celesta(1936); his *Sonata for Two Pianos and Per-cussion* (1937); his *Violin Concerto* (1938); and his *Divertimento* (1939) stand as marks of proof.

These latter four works have much in common; above all a purified simplicity, perhaps the most com-pact, timeless valid formulation of the period's bitter fears and threatening anxieties. At the same time, they contain an affinity to the classical method of structure. The works lead from the first movements' philosophi-cal exposition of the theme through shattering, bitter moods and thoughts into the last movements' resol-ution with folk-music elements. The last movements reverberate with an unbroken faith, an unrestrained determination, and even an elevated, strict serenity rising above the horrors of the moment. This is well illustrated in the central piece of Bartók's opus, perhaps even in all artistic achievements of the time, the *Music for Strings, Percussion and Celesta*, which was first performed on January 21, 1937. If we were to seek one piece of music to illustrate this historical period (even if it is futile to attempt to translate music into pictures or thoughts) I should venture to say that there is hardly a more fitting work. Few compositions could create more artistically polarised moods of sound – through contrasting the catastrophic, elemen-tal explosion of the kettle drum's rising *fortissimo* and falling *pianissimo* with the transcendentally pure tone of the celesta. The threatening roll of the kettle drums floats into a dancing folk melody, the piano solo, first subdued, then striking with unexpected harshness and accompanied by a rumbling thunder of drums, are sounds which evoke the mood of the time. The true contrast is perhaps not as much in this as in the episodes of unperturbed harmony, folk-song-like carelessness suddenly changing to unexpected haste, a wild rush and a pursuit of clashing rhythms – to be again resolved in attainment. The sobbing, lamenting melodies, the terror of themes dying in the snapping of strings and the wrestling forces of dancing rhythms finally dissolve in the spiteful clarity of the leit-motif and the almost reverent, elevated hymns at the finish. The motifs, based on folk-song elements and radiating a solid, serene faith, find harmonic significance in this music.

Béla Bartók's deliberate musical programme grew out of a desire to contribute to the solving of important social and political questions. In private life he was very far removed from politics, in a sense even apolitical, a sensitive and reserved artist. Yet, he made a (for him) unusually passionate, even pathos-laden confession, and it is, perhaps, not insignificant in that age of national hatred that he did this in a letter to Octavian Beu of Bucharest:

My true governing ideal, however, which since I have found myself as a composer I am totally aware of, is the ideal of the brotherhood of peoples – brotherhood, in spite of all war and conflict. This ideal I try to serve in my music as much as I can; for this reason I will not withdraw from any influence, be it of Slovak, Rumanian, Arabic or any other source. Only it must be a clear, fresh and wholesome source![28]

Bartók's music, rupturing, unsettling and thought-provoking, is bitter and sensitively nervous, as were all the greatest artistic accomplishments of the period; yet, at the same time, it is filled with faith. Behind it stands a musical programme and a belief in the brotherhood of, and the possibility of the fruitful encounter between, peoples. It is in this that he becomes a representative of East-Central European thought. Erupting playfully, pure joy finds expression even among burdened anguish, even in the folk-song based, increasingly turbulent, very bitter orchestral concerto's closing movement, which might be regarded as a summary of his life's work. Even in the depressing atmosphere of the time, Béla Bartók believed in the values of humanity and of peoples, as did Thomas Mann, Berthold Brecht, Ceslav Miłos, Miloslav Krleža, Joseph Sima and so many others. They tried to defend those values and fought for them to the end.

The artistic resistance fed and guarded the flame which not even the most ferocious devastation of Nazism could put out, and which awakening mankind could at the price of great sacrifice make grow into the fire of triumph.

Notes

1 Galbraith, J. K. *The Age of Uncertainty*, pp. 133–4, Boston, 1977.

2 Bukharin, N. *Imperialism and World Economy*, p. 21, New York and London, 1973.

3 Davis, H. W. C. *The Political Thought of Heinrich von Treitschke*, pp. 105–6, London, 1914.

4 Fichte, J. G. *Der geschlossene Handelsstaat. Ein philosophischer Entwurf als Anhang zur Rectslehre und Probe einer künftig zur liefernden Politik*, pp. 17, 68, Jena, 1920. Quoted by Butler, R. D'O. *The Roots of National Socialism 1783–1933*, p. 37, London, 1941.

5 Fichte, J. G. *Der geschlossene Handelsstaat. Ein philosophischer Entwurf als Anhang zur Rectslehre und Probe einer künftig zur liefernden Politik*, pp. 35, 97, Jena, 1920. Quoted by Butler, R. D'O. *The Roots of National Socialism 1783–1933*, p. 38, London, 1941.

6 *The Fascist Era*. Published by the Fascist Confederation of Industrialists, Rome, 1939. Quoted by Arendt, H. *The Origin of Totalitarianism*, p. 258, Cleveland, New York, 1958.

7 Zelea Codreanu, C. *For My Legionnaires. The Iron Guard*, pp. 304–9, Madrid, 1976.

8 Zelea Codreanu, C. *For My Legionnaires. The Iron Guard*, p. 312, Madrid, 1976.

9 Sternhall, Z. *Fascist Ideology*. In Laqueur (ed.) *Fascism: A Reader's Guide. Analyses, Interpretation, Bibliography*, p. 339, New York, 1979.

10 Moholy-Nagy, S. *Moholy-Nagy. Experiment in totality*, p. 13, Cambridge (Ma) and London, 1969.

11 Moholy-Nagy, S. *Moholy-Nagy. Experiment in Totality*, pp. 114–15, Cambridge (MA) and London, 1969.

12 Korbel, J. *Twentieth Century Czechoslovakia*, pp. 52, 60, New York, 1977.

13 Rothschild, J. *Pilsudski's Coup d'etat*, p. 118; New York, 1966.

14 Freud, S. *Autobiography*, p. 11, New York, 1935.

15 Weber, E. *Revolution? Counter-revolution? What Revolution?* in Laqueur (ed.) *Fascism: A Reader's Guide. Analyses, Interpretation, Bibliography*, p. 503, New York, 1979.

16 Kogan, N. *Fascism as a Political System*. In Woolf, J. S. (ed.) *The Nature of Fascism*, p. 13, London, 1968.

17 Mosse, G. *The Crisis of German Ideology. Intellectual Origins of the Reich*, p. 292, London, 1966.

18 Hinz, B. *Art in the Third Reich*, pp. 27–8, Oxford, 1979.

19 Hinz, B. *Art in the Third Reich*, p. 15, Oxford, 1979.

20 Leisen, E. *Nazi Cinema*, p. 34, New York, 1975.

21 Baynes, N. H. (ed.) *The Speeches of Adolf Hitler, April 1922 – August 1939. Vol. 1*, p. 567, London, New York, Toronto, 1942.

22 Baynes, N. H. (ed.) *The Speeches of Adolf Hitler, April 1922 – August 1939. Vol. 1*, p. 78, London, New York, Toronto, 1942.

23 Hinz, B. *Art in the Third Reich*, pp. 78–9, Oxford, 1979.

24 Speer, A. *Inside the Third Reich. Memoirs*, p. 103, New York, 1970.

25 Speer, A. *Inside the Third Reich. Memoirs*, p. 69, New York, 1970.

26 Bálint, Gy. *A toronyör visszapillant. The Guard Looks Back. Vol. 2*, pp. 279–80, Budapest, 1961.

27 Holländer, H. *Die Musik in der Kulturgeschichte des 19. und 20. Jahrhunderts*, p. 19, Köln, 1967.

28 Béla Bartók's *Selected Letters*, p. 397, Budapest, 1976.

Index

101

Index

Index

Index

DATE DUE

CAYLORD